Government Performan

PUBLISHING FOR THE WORLD
125 Years
THE JOHNS HOPKINS UNIVERSITY PRESS

Johns Hopkins Studies in Governance and Public Management
Kenneth J. Meier and Laurence J. O'Toole Jr., Series Editors

Government Performance
Why Management Matters

PATRICIA W. INGRAHAM
PHILIP G. JOYCE
AMY KNEEDLER DONAHUE

The Johns Hopkins University Press
BALTIMORE AND LONDON

© 2003 The Johns Hopkins University Press
All rights reserved. Published 2003
Printed in the United States of America on acid-free paper
9 8 7 6 5 4 3 2 1

The Johns Hopkins University Press
2715 North Charles Street
Baltimore, Maryland 21218-4363
www.press.jhu.edu

Library of Congress Cataloging-in-Publication Data
Ingraham, Patricia W.
Government performance : why management matters / Patricia W. Ingraham,
Philip G. Joyce, Amy Kneedler Donahue.
    p.   cm. — (Johns Hopkins studies in governance and public management)
Includes bibliographical references and index.
ISBN 0-8018-7227-8 (hard : alk. paper)
ISBN 0-8018-7228-6 (pbk. : alk. paper)
1. Public administration—United States. 2. Administrative agencies—United States—
Management. I. Joyce, Philip G., 1956– II. Donahue, Amy Kneedler, 1966– III. Title.
IV. Series.
JK421 .I54 2003
352.3′0973—dc21
2002009869

A catalog record for this book is available from the British Library.

To our families, without whose love, support, and distractions neither the projects nor the book would have been possible.

Contents

Figures and Tables

Figures

Tables

Series Editors' Foreword

The Johns Hopkins Studies in Governance and Public Management seeks to publish the best empirically oriented work at the junction of public policy and public management. The goal is to build knowledge that can make a difference in how we understand public policies and that can make their operation more effective. The Johns Hopkins Studies in Governance and Public Management take a special interest in the problems of governance and performance, including managerial issues linked to institutional arrangements, policy instruments, human resources, and finance. The series reflects the increased interest in these subjects not only in the United States but also in other developed democracies. The Studies are distinguished by the use of diverse, sophisticated, and innovative methods; and they are expected to make important and enduring theoretical contributions.

This first study, by Patricia Ingraham, Philip Joyce, and Amy Kneedler Donahue, fits squarely into these interests and developments. The authors led the Government Performance Project (GPP), supported by The Pew Charitable Trusts, over several years of activity at the Campbell Institute of Public Affairs, The Maxwell School, Syracuse University, with portions of the work undertaken at The George Washington University as well. As readers of such publications as *Governing* and *Government Executive* are well aware, the GPP undertook the ambitious task of assessing the public management capacity of many federal agencies, state governments, and large cities and counties. The results have included highly publicized evaluations of managerial systems and overall management capacity as well as detailed qualitative information about nuanced features across many governments.

Although GPP-generated data on agencies' and governments' scores have been published in various outlets during the last couple of years, this book provides the overall report of the full project, including its conceptualization, design, and methods; a considerable number of its findings; and detailed exploration of its implications for both research and practice.

Ingraham, Joyce, and Donahue frame the assessment of governmental performance within an explicit model of management capacity and its components. Experts and practicing managers are convinced that the quality of public-managerial systems makes a significant difference in how well governments deliver on their commitments, and most are convinced as well that agencies and governments vary greatly in managerial capacity. Ingraham and her colleagues add important substantive content to these generalizations. They identify a set of specific components that comprise managerial capacity, and they specify how these components should integrate if governments are to optimize in their managerial efforts.

In a careful and detailed fashion, the authors work from the assumption that the relevant experts in different public-managerial specialties possess valid knowledge about managerial capacity. As a result of systematic data gathering from such experts, the authors develop detailed assessment criteria incorporating such managerial elements as workforce planning, systematic revenue forecasting, and managing for results. They then report on the results of their exhaustive data-gathering efforts across federal, state, and local governments and provide a clear and often encouraging portrait of the managerial capacity of contemporary American government.

The focus of this study is on a particular part of what the authors call the governmental "performance equation." Their intent is to see if knowledgeable experts agree on the content of management capacity (the authors find considerable agreement) and also to report on extensive data from a range of agencies and governments in order to assess systematically how they compare to these consensus standards. The influence of these features on the ultimate performance of governments in the United States is not an issue examined in detail here, although the authors have developed some strong hunches about the causal links that are worth systematic attention. While it can be left to others to examine the links between management capacity and the outputs and outcomes of government policy, the authors establish a set of standards for conceptualization, measurement, and comparison. This contribution is no mean feat, and this book clearly advances our understanding of critical elements of governance and public management.

Kenneth J. Meier and Laurence J. O'Toole Jr.

Preface

The Government Performance Project (GPP) and the Federal Performance Project (FPP) described in this book were big and unwieldy. They tackled very tough problems and questions. They set out to measure and compare functions and activities of government not only in new ways but in ways that were easily understandable and communicated. They required cooperation and partnership between universities, between academics and journalists, and between overworked public employees and those who wished to analyze them. There were political issues, management issues, state of knowledge issues, and profound fairness and legitimacy issues. And there was a five-year timetable to demonstrate that management was important to governments' capacity for performance and that governments themselves cared about the links.

No activity of this scope is possible without the help and cooperation of many people. That was undeniably the case with the GPP and the FPP. We relied on friends, experts, students, and government officials for advice, support, and assistance. Although in the beginning we often "relied on the kindness of strangers," by projects' end we believed that many of those strangers had become part of a broad and positive community. We hope that we have not forgotten anyone in the thanks that follow; we apologize if we have.

We extend special thanks to The Pew Charitable Trusts, not only for their support of the projects but for the remarkable vision of well-publicized accountability measures for government that created the projects' partnerships. The Trusts mandated that the Government Performance Project—initially covering all levels of government—"prove" itself in the pilot year. To that end, it was carefully monitored for performance and quality by an advisory board. The board, chaired by Senator Mark O. Hatfield, was enormously helpful. The board's collective experience and wisdom and Senator Hatfield's exceptional guidance were critical to getting off to a good start.

Government Performance Project

Amy Schmit, the GPP's first project director, was called the Goddess of the GPP—for very good reasons. Her enthusiasm, energy, and remarkable skills were hallmarks of the GPP's first two years and created the firm foundation that allowed successful completion of what sometimes appeared to be never-ending tasks. The student teams that Amy organized and managed for project support achieved the nearly impossible and did so with humor and good will. Anthony Stacy and Jessica Crawford continued Amy's tradition of excellence for the GPP. Dale Jones assumed the position of director of the overall GPP for the second state round and for the county round. His guidance was vital to the project's success in that period. Bethany Walawender was the budget guru, in the very best sense of the term. At times when we wondered how to hold it all together, angels appeared, including Robin Rhoades, Janet Pryzborski, and Kelley Coleman.

Each year MPA and doctoral students from the Maxwell School joined the GPP team. The full list of the MPA students—the "Campbell Crew," as they dubbed themselves—is included in the Appendix. Every crew member made important and lasting contributions to the project. They produced consistently high quality work while also maintaining excellent academic records, often by working around the clock. They also made us laugh and took funny pictures. We can never thank them enough.

The doctoral students deserve special mention not only for becoming the institutional memory of the project as they completed their doctoral work but also for the expertise they applied to the management systems they studied. Don Moynihan and Ora-Orn Poocharoen shepherded the managing for results analyses at Maxwell. Willow Jacobson took the lead in human resource management. Yilin Hou did outstanding work on financial management. Both Don's and Yilin's dissertations emerged from GPP work.

For commitment, for quality, and—again—for good humor, these students were top notch.

The journalists from *Governing* magazine spent countless hours interviewing state and local officials, participating in the grading process, and distilling the results for public consumption. *Governing's* editor and publisher, Peter Harkness, and managing editor, Alan Ehrenhalt, contributed their extensive talents to the project as well.

We also thank the expert advisors and the faculty experts for their contributions—too numerous to list—to the project content and quality. Pages could be written about the ways in which these experts shaped and assisted the project and its many levels of analysis. We ask them to forgive us for simply listing their names and institutions: John Bartle, B. J. Reid, Carol Ebdon, and Dale Krane from the University of Nebraska at Omaha provided excellent lead faculty assistance, as did Bill Duncombe from the Maxwell

School and Sally Selden from Lynchberg College. Hal Rainey and Larry O'Toole from the University of Georgia played key advising roles. During her time at the Maxwell School, Astrid Merget provided constant moral support—a resource critical to the undertaking. Michaela Buhler and Polly Dement, our public relations guides and leaders, were exemplars of expertise and classy hard work. The coverage they obtained for the project and the seriousness with which the results were covered nationwide were important measures of success.

Federal Performance Project

The federal portion of the project was conducted separately from the state and local side, both when the entire project was at Maxwell and when the federal portion of the project migrated to The George Washington University. Over the entire period, the staff at *Government Executive* magazine, led by Tim Clark, used their considerable experience and journalistic talents to uncover many examples of good and bad management in federal agencies. Equally important, they followed the required protocols imposed on them by academic colleagues (such as interviewing the same kinds of people and asking the same kinds of questions) with skill and good humor. Of particular note are the contributions of Anne Laurent, deputy editor of *Government Executive*—the project was not her idea, but she took it on as if it were, and her tough questions and high standards are as responsible as anything for the high quality of the project.

On the academic side, in addition to the Maxwell staff already noted above, Professor Joyce was blessed with excellent support from graduate students and faculty at The George Washington University. A full listing of the students is included in the Appendix, but it should be noted here that the Master's students distinguished themselves and their institution by working long hours and largely creating order out of chaos by summarizing huge amounts of information. The project manager at The George Washington University, Howard Smith, worked tirelessly and coupled his considerable knowledge from years of experience in the General Accounting Office (GAO) and in the private sector with insights gained as a Ph.D. student to develop a smooth process for collecting and evaluating information on the federal agencies studied. The other faculty in the Department of Public Administration, particularly department chair Kathy Newcomer, provided both intellectual and operational support; GWU has proved a good "home" for the project.

Finally, many people in the vast community of individuals concerned with federal management issues contributed to the quality of the project (but should not be held responsible for its shortcomings). We consulted a number of external advisors at various stages of the process. They are too numerous to list here (we do list them in the Appendix), but some deserve special mention. Mort Downey was an early and enthusiastic supporter of the project, both early on when he was deputy secretary of the Department of Transportation (DOT) and later when he served on our Grading Advisory Panel. Ed DeSeve was likewise very helpful in this latter capacity, but also notably when he was deputy director for management at the Office of Management and Budget (OMB). Jonathan Breul from OMB and Chris Mihm from GAO, on anybody's short list of managing for results gurus in the federal government, provided helpful and consistent intellectual support, while at the same time keeping us honest.

For both the GPP and the FPP, however, perhaps the most important thanks go to the governments and agencies that contributed their time and expertise in providing the information we needed to complete the analysis. The overwhelming majority of the governments involved participated, if not with joy, with great dedication. They demonstrated a commitment to learning and to the quality of government that cynics had assured us would not be present. We were never able to give them enough in return; the pace of the project moved us on to another level of government or set of agencies before the last round of analysis had really settled in. We thank these hundreds of public employees for their generous help and for their many insights into how and why good management matters to good government. We hope that this book slightly decreases our debt to them.

Government Performance

1 | Management, Capacity, and Performance

Efficient. Productive. High performing. These are all powerful symbolic terms when applied to government. But well managed? High capacity? How do these terms fit into the debate? Are they even part of the debate about how to improve the daily business of government and the performance of public organizations?

For the past century the government reform debate has allowed efficiency and performance reforms ample time in the sun. Often the objectives are presented in tandem, as in the efficiency and productivity movements in the early 1920s and 1930s. (For classic statements of the tenets central to these movements, see Taylor, 1911; Gulick and Urwick, 1937). Sometimes they are presented as contrasts to the reality of government, as in the National Performance Review's assertion that in a government where "process is our most important product" performance necessarily suffers (NPR, 1993b). The ideal has nearly always been the perceived performance of private sector organizations.

Frequent cycles of change, considerable confusion about the intent of reform, and scant attention to the public context of efficiency, productivity, and now performance, have, however, caused political and public disillusionment with the ability of government organizations to change. Many reforms have been deemed failures. (For a set of perspectives, see Ingraham, 1995; Light, 1997). Nonetheless, reform efforts continue. Most recently, performance-centered reforms have had primacy. Managing for results, performance-based budgeting, the Government Performance and Results Act (1993), and other efforts reflect an emphasis on the outputs and outcomes of government programs and activities. In a closely related development, *process*—a term that nicely summarizes the legal and procedural environments in which most public organizations operate—has been cast as a negative force.

However the debate has been cast, a critical component remains largely unexamined. Management—its qualities, processes, and activities—has been taken for granted. Of course management matters, both scholars and practitioners have asserted, and there is no need to pursue the issue further. But *how* does management matter? *When* does it matter? If it matters in a negative way, can it be fixed? Is management a neutral, technical activity, as many of the assumptions that underpin civil service systems suggest, or is it something far more complex that profoundly affects governments' abilities to deliver the promise of government to citizens?

The fundamental argument of this book is that effective management is basic to the overall effectiveness of government. How it matters and when it matters are clearly fertile grounds for future analysis and theory building. This necessary exploration, however, must proceed from the premise that what managers and management systems do inside public organizations and how they do it have an impact on how public organizations are able to perform. The linkage is important and central; its exploration is long overdue.

How management matters is of particular importance now because performance has become a mantra for reformers and analysts at all levels of government. The conditions for effective performance—the platforms for performance—have not been fully considered, however. Common sense tells us that unless threshold conditions for effective performance are present, emphasizing outcomes and measuring performance are likely to be dispiriting exercises. Rhetoric and inflated expectations have frequently obscured this commonsense link, however, and in that sense, have seriously limited the chance for successful reform.

Let us be clear: we assume that management activities and systems do not exist as ends in themselves but as one part of the complex capacity-building link to performance in public organizations. At the same time, the arguments advanced in the following chapters make the claim that management matters in ways that are central to public performance. All else being equal, if public organizations have good managers and good management systems, we assume that they are more likely to be effective performers. But it is important not to construe the development of such management capacity as demonstrated performance. Capacity is, rather, a *platform* for performance —a measure of positive or negative potential to obtain desired program results and policy outcomes. Similarly, it is a mistake to consider performance and measurement of performance in a context that does not also include analysis of capacity to perform.

This last point is significant. The role of measurement in the public performance equation—the linkage between resources, management, and results—has been the focus of a large literature. It is an enormously complex issue. Research related to service delivery and performance measurement is extensive, sophisticated, and increasingly cumulative. (For an excellent summary of key literature, see Lynn, Heinrich, and Hill, 1999.) There is good evidence that performance measures and performance information are becoming one part of policy decision making in many governments (Barrett and Greene, 1999). Certainly, that is the intent of the Government Performance and Results Act at the federal level and of many managing for results programs in states and cities.

An exclusive focus on input or outcome measurement without consideration of the context of, and the capacity for, performance can, however, be both misleading and destructive in the public sector. The primary reason for this is straightforward: overly simple measures do not convey the substantial complexity of the performance system they strive to represent. It is frequently asserted, for example, that citizens do not really care about how well government works; they care about trash collection, clean streets, and good police protection. All of these are, of course, part of good government. Cost and efficiency of delivery measures are important and are probably also the easiest pieces of information to collect, but they are only a part of what citizens and elected officials need to know. Also critical is information about how well governments use resources available to them, about how they balance and trade off competing citizen demands and needs, about the quality and timeliness of the information they use to make decisions and where they get it, and about the commitment of government and its leaders to effective service. Again, the link to capacity is apparent: governments and their managers cannot do what citizens and elected officials ask if they lack the fundamental ability or capacity to deliver. In short, we assume that management is a crucial antecedent to programmatic outputs and policy outcomes. This book therefore has as its core focus the nature of effective management; it does not examine outcome measures. The intent is to create and apply measures that accurately reflect the *management capacity* of federal, state, and local governments to make the point clearer.

At a symposium on performance, an academic analyst urged: "Let's all make a pledge to . . . stop asking 'Does management matter?' because of course it matters. The questions are how, when, and under what conditions it matters. Let's get the questions right."* Amen. But getting the questions right is only the first step. The more difficult step is to reach an understanding of how, precisely, answers to the questions lead to a better understanding of performance and to the links between well-managed organizations and better performance. The following chapters make that effort. But first, some consideration of previous efforts to "get the questions right" is necessary.

*Comments by Janet Weiss at the workshop on Models and Methods for the Empirical Study of Governance, held at the Eller School Business and Public Policy, University of Arizona, April 29–May 1, 1999.

"Management Is Neutral"

The link between management and performance has been made, although not always explicitly, for many years. The specific ties between good administration and efficiency created by the scientific administration theorists, for example, were straightforward. Administration, to be effective, had to focus on technique and technical skills; it had to be removed from "policy" in the political decision-making sense of the term, and efficiency objectives had to take priority (W. Wilson, 1887; White, 1926; Goodnow, 1900). Administration needed to focus all of its energies and resources on efficient achievement of goals and objectives. Straying from that focus produced inefficiency. Therefore, Woodrow Wilson's (1887) argument that good administration could "straighten the path of government" had implications not only for politics but for long-term government performance as well.

At the same time, the argument of these theorists that administration was a neutral activity—a "hammer or a saw," as Kaufman (1965) put it—placed the activity in an anomalous and not altogether comfortable situation. Effective administration *could* lead to greater efficiency and productivity, but only if the administrative process itself was sterilized. (To be fair, most theorists in this group also clearly recognized that concern for equity was a critical component of public organizational life). Lynn (1996) argues that this perspective was effectively "finished off" by post–World War II theorists who noted that policy and policy decisions were open and fluid and that elected officials were as likely to worry about policy implementation as about policy design. Perhaps. There is, however, a disconcerting similarity between the walling of policy from administration in the early theories and the separation of "steering" from "rowing" in recent reinvention literature. (For a discussion of the various components of reinventing government, see Kettl, 1994.)

Many analyses of the effectiveness of specific public policies—and of the relationships between elected officials and public managers—continue to operate with the explicit assumption that the relationship can be distortion-free, or rational. Principal-agent theory as applied to public bureaucracy, for example, assumes that, given proper direction and constraints, the bureaucratic agent will respond in a neutral way to a principal's purpose (see Wood and Peak, 1998). Terry Moe states the problem quite explicitly when he notes that principal-agent models view public organizations as "black boxes that mysteriously mediate between interests and outcomes. The implicit claim is that institutions do not matter much" (1987:475).* At the same time, one of the assumptions lurking in many of the analyses to which Moe refers is that *controlling* bureaucratic institutions and actors is critical to effective policy. The conundrum clearly suggests the need for more in-depth analysis of the bureaucratic role.

Management as Professional Leadership and Guidance

Another possible approach to specifying linkages between management and performance is provided by a group of theorists who draw distinctions between *management* and *administration* (Waldo, 1955; Lynn, 1996). As Evans and Wamsley (1999) observe, this has created substantial conceptual confusion. It has also created an uncertainty about who and what in public management is most deserving of focus and analysis. At the same time, some of this careful work has made a serious contribution to better specification of the policy/performance equation and to public management's placement in it (Lynn, Heinrich, and Hill, 1999). There are three notable dimensions here. The first is the definition of the role of public managers as decision makers, strategists, and analysts rather than as neutral technocrats (Lynn, 1996). The second is the somewhat contradictory but enduring confidence in analysis and measurement as neutral activities. The third is the effort to move away from the institutions of government and management (the more traditional public administration perspective) to an emphasis on leadership, key transactions, and individual managerial skills and abilities. Evans and Wamsley (1999) argue that this last movement necessarily implies a focus on political leadership rather than on the career bureaucracy.

All of these dimensions are useful to exploring links between management and performance. They are connected by a common theme of proactive management; they emphasize that management and leadership activities play an important shaping role both inside and outside the organization; and they explicitly argue that the organizations and the systems with which we are concerned are amenable to structured analysis. In policy management terms, many public management theorists have moved from a view of administration as a passive, neutral "black box" to one that accepts a substantial and

---

*Moe (1987) contains an analysis of the general perspective, which was strongly reiterated in his presentation the 2001 Annual Meeting of the American Political Science Association, San Francisco, Calif., August 30–September 2, 2001.

legitimate role in shaping public policy. Moreover, recent analyses have contributed to a better understanding of how to begin the dissection of structural, organizational, and managerial impacts on broader policy outcomes (Meyers and Dillon, 1999; Sandfort, 2000). Much of this work has focused on the implementation of specific public policies.

In this book, we do not study implementation per se. Because we focus on *management capacity development*—the middle of the performance equation described more fully in the next chapter—we analyze a government's potential to translate resources into public policy products. We examine whether governments have the capacity, the people, and the systems to be effective implementers and whether they know how to fix it if they are not. In that sense, we view effective management as an intervening influence both on effective implementation and on longer-term performance. Nonetheless, recent implementation findings have important implications for the arguments we advance. To clarify how the models we present both draw upon and differ from those advanced in existing implementation literature, it is useful to examine key findings of recent research.

Management, Implementation, and Performance

Far from viewing management in neutral terms, early implementation theorists viewed it as a powerful influence. The work of Pressman and Wildavsky (1984), for example, assigned a generally distorting and negative impact to the role of bureaucrats and managers. Their argument was, essentially, that cramming diffuse policy objectives into standardized bureaucratic boxes and processes created a product virtually unrecognizable from the original. Other early analyses emphasized the impact of loosely linked legislative objectives and bureaucratic processes on policy redefinition (Nakamura and Smallwood, 1980). All recognized the impact of the profoundly political environment of implementation on the nature of the activity itself as well as on eventual policy performance. To the extent that management was recognized in these analyses, it was as a nearly constant problem-solving activity, whose effect was largely unpredictable but whose overall influence was substantial.

More recent work has analyzed the impacts of structure and structural differentiation on implementation. The concept of networks of relationships within and across public organizations and levels of government appropriately captures the complexity of modern organizations and their internal and external environments (Mandell, 1990; O'Toole, 1996). The research also introduces important new questions about the conditions under which implementation can be effective and about the criteria or judgments against which such effectiveness should be assessed (Provan and Milward, 1995).

Perhaps the most important emerging finding is awareness of the inadequacy of relying on organizations as units of analysis. Effective implementation and performance requires a network-wide cooperation and integration strategy. Common objectives must flow throughout the network; in fact, they bind the network together in important ways. As this literature evolves, the ideas of communication, coordination, and integration become central. Provan and Milward are unequivocal: "The basic building block of any network study is the linkages among the organizations that make up the network" (1995: 10). This emphasis on coordination and integration is central to the conceptualization of the research described in this book.

This emerging research in networks and effectiveness also encounters methodological problems related to those we describe later in this book. Simply put, network theorists assume that structure and level of integration of the system influence outcomes. This is similar to our assumption that management capacity and effectiveness have a long-term influence on performance. There is, in fact, a substantive connection between the use of the term *integration* in the network research, and the term *capacity development* used in the research described here. As later chapters demonstrate, while we rely on integration as only one dimension of capacity in our research, our concept of potential for performance is very similar to the network theorist's concept of potential effectiveness. Despite the current paucity of empirical evidence that fully supports either assumption, both have a commonsense foundation as well as evidence that points to further exploration.

In earlier work, we noted that the current state of interorganizational scholarship "hints at an emerging empirical relationship between the study of policy implementation by public agencies, the refinement of formal models of bureaucracy, and the development of theories of integrated service network behavior and effectiveness" (Ingraham and Kneedler, 2000a: 240). A key but currently absent link in the study of these policies, organizations, and systems is management. The failure to specify what is essentially the middle of the performance equation seriously hampers both empirical analysis and practical efforts at change and reform.

Leaders, Managers, and Management Systems

Linking management to performance also requires specification of what it is about management that is likely to influence effectiveness in the long term. The organizational network theory cited above has moved away from organizations as the critical unit of analysis. In our work, we add another dimension to that departure. We argue that a key and essentially unexplored quality of management is the nature of the systems created to support and advance management activity. Again, a disclaimer is necessary: in emphasizing management systems, we do not discount the role of individuals, nor do we argue that systems are the only organizational characteristic worthy of analysis. We clearly do not, for example, discount the pivotal role that leaders and leadership play in shaping and directing organizational resources (Behn, 1991; Lynn, 1996). In fact, one of the conclusions that we describe later is that leaders and leadership teams appear key to effective capacity development.

We do argue, however, that in any institutional setting it is necessary to consider the devices and processes that translate leaders' visions and goal into substantive action. This is not magic; it is a process that mandates consistent and predictable support. Furthermore, as leaders come and go— and they do—government cannot and does not stop. The institutional bases for continued effectiveness are the management systems that have been imbedded within and across governments and agencies. These systems allow organizations to hire and fire, to spend, to build, to provide services, and to collect information crucial to all of these efforts. While leaders and top managers can shape these systems in important ways, the systems can also support or constrain the ability of leaders to be successful.

Finally, we note that, in continuing efforts to reform and improve the management capacity and performance of government, the identification of malleable points of change is central to success. While leadership may be changed at the polls, the systems that support their activities in office are rarely the topic of debate. Yet they are change levers: they can be changed by legislation, by judicial actions, by internal managerial decisions, and by leaders' fiat. We argue that paying attention to the quality and alignment of these management systems is an important step toward improved performance. Is it the only important step? Obviously not. We argue simply for its inclusion in the overall performance debate.

The Government and Federal Performance Projects

This book presents and explains the conceptual foundation, methods, and findings of two extensive examinations of government management. The Government Performance Project (GPP) and the Federal Performance Project (FPP) are five-year studies funded by The Pew Charitable Trusts. They are comprehensive descriptive analyses of public management systems in all fifty states, the thirty-five largest cities, forty large counties, and twenty-seven federal agencies. The states were surveyed twice; some of the federal agencies were more informally revisited.

Operating from the base assumption that management systems provide critical support to individual leaders and managers and also provide important crosscutting integrative abilities, the research examines four systems in depth: financial management, human resources management, information technology management, and capital management. These systems and the criteria-based assessment used in this research are described in greater detail in Chapter 3. In our view, these systems represent critical elements of management capabilities. Three other dimensions—leadership, integration, and systems for managing for results—are also included in the analysis. All are very important to public agencies, where leadership is provided by elected and appointed officials as well as by members of the career public service, where integration often means crossing or eliminating legislative and institutional boundaries, and where a focus on results can serve to make legislative and executive priorities concrete.

The research and the view of management presented in the following chapters are based on intensive analysis of the management systems of the governments noted above. This analysis is primarily descriptive. Our key intents are to carefully identify the consensus of knowledgeable experts about what constitutes management capacity, to gather extensive data about management systems and behaviors from a range of agencies and governments in the United States, and to assess systematically how they compare to these consensus standards. Data were gathered from three major sources: an extensive self-administered written survey sent to the governments and agencies studied; numerous follow-up interviews by experienced journalists about the survey results; and analysis of a multitude of reports, plans, and other documents related to management systems, activities, and performance. This book summarizes the most comprehensive examination of government management systems ever undertaken.

The Structure of the Book

Our discussion to this point has emphasized the need to include management and management systems in the broader discussion of building capacity for governments and agencies to perform. In earlier work, we outlined a preliminary conceptual model to clarify some of the key points of our argument (Ingraham and Kneedler, 2000a). In this book, we take a different approach. The data gathered now allow fuller exposition about some of the assumptions on which we relied earlier; they permit a building-block learning approach to the study of the role of management in a variety of settings.

We analyze the two key questions that underpin our research—Can "good" management be defined and described? How does management build capacity and contribute to performance? We begin, not with a model that we assume to be correct, but with an iterative process that will lead to identification of key components of such a model and serve as a launch pad for future research. Although the variables and characteristics included in the earlier discussions were the product of extensive literature reviews and expert advising, their empirical foundation was limited. In this book, we are able to move beyond that constraint. In the process, some factors earlier identified as important emerge as less so; others have been added. Indeed, the complexity of the research questions has sometimes been overwhelming. Despite our best efforts, the following chapters cannot fully capture the richness we found.

We also recognize that, even as we achieve a better ability to answer questions about how and when management makes a difference to performance, a key set of research activities remain. Management is a necessarily intervening influence on program outputs and outcomes, but our intent here is not to examine those links in a specific case. Instead, we hope by the end of the book to have clarified how management might be included in such future analyses. In short, we create a set of standards for conceptualization, measurement, and comparison. Later research may be able to use this work to probe various parts of the performance equation, and we have developed some strong insights about which kinds of causal links are particularly worth systematic attention. Our purpose here is to begin what we know will be a much longer process.

We begin in Chapter 2 with a fuller discussion of the ways in which management may be explored and described. We describe our methodological approaches to assessing the components of management and management systems and to presenting results. We conclude with chapters on major lessons learned and on substantive directions for future work.

In this chapter, we sought to make the case that management must be included in the discussion of broader performance and in reform activities that seek to improve performance. We explored some past efforts to make the linkages we study here. Chapter 2 addresses the question of operationalizing management. As we noted earlier, four common core management systems are financial management, human resources management, capital management, and information technology management. Two other factors are also significant: the extent to which government organizations focus on results, and the extent to which management systems are integrated and mutually supportive. In addition, leadership is assumed to play important integration and change initiation roles. This chapter introduces and explains the concept of management capacity, which captures the extent to which administrative functions successfully marshal government's financial, human, capital, and information resources to enhance effectiveness and performance. In sum, the chapter and the model it contains attempt to demonstrate how management capacity can be a key link between public resources and public results.

Chapter 3 explains the criteria-based assessment approach used to assess government management and describes the activities and processes that led to the choice of the criteria utilized in the GPP and FPP. Chapter 4 presents our methodology and the techniques we used to gather information about management and to assess the extent to which criteria were met. These were elaborate and complicated methods, involving both in-depth academic analysis and interpretive journalistic assessments. The final results—the grades chosen as the summary measures in these studies—were products of the same collaboration.

Chapter 5 presents the results of the GPP: the state- and local-level findings, and the conclusions of the research to date. These include conclusions about management quality generally, but we also discuss each of the core management systems. Specific case examples are included as well as broad general conclusions. In Chapter 6 we present our findings for the federal agencies we examined in year 1 of the GPP and in the FPP thereafter. Again, specific examples as well as broad general lessons are included. In Chapter 7 we present broad crosscutting lessons learned: how and under what circumstances we believe that management matters and when it seems to matter most, the critical role played by leadership, and the building-block strategy for developing capacity. The discussion clearly places management in the broader capacity-building and performance debates that now underpin many efforts at public change and reform.

The final chapter maps future needs. Despite a spate of recent research, some using GPP data, clear links between good management and specific performance results must still be forged. Of equal significance, the findings of this and related research about how and why management matters must be incorporated into future discussions of reform and into shaping expectations for future change. Better understanding and more careful creation of platforms for performance in government are vital. Citizen expectations for improved performance and effectiveness in government activities are better served by creating real potential to deliver on public promises than by empty promises. And the very real levers for change and long-term policy success that management systems and reforms to them represent should not be ignored.

Public managers and management systems are emerging as important components in the larger realm of governance, where collective decisions about public policy are linked to governmental activity.* As governments move toward greater emphasis on results, they and their constituents have sought improved government performance, as evidenced by the modern reform efforts discussed in Chapter 1. Many contingencies that critically influence government performance, such as elections, socioeconomic conditions, media scrutiny, legislative priorities, and social perception of the scope and scale of policy problems, are beyond the control of public organizations and their managers. In addition, legislative mandates often dictate—and constrain—the very structure of government organizations. Nonetheless, public management does influence considerably the approaches governments and their agencies use to orchestrate resources and translate them into public services. Thus, in order to understand how to improve public performance, we argue that those components of performance that public managers do substantially control must receive prime attention.

This chapter presents the conceptual framework that supports the GPP and FPP efforts to describe management and to discover how management can be assessed. Because the goal is to develop a comprehensive and valid evaluation of government management, we must create and apply measures of public entities' ability to effectively acquire, sustain, maintain, and deploy an administrative infrastructure that supports their desired service outcomes. In other words, we must characterize a key intervening variable in the classic model that relates resources to results: government management. Understanding the "black box" that traditionally has been used to depict government management necessitates resolving management into its con-

---

*In their recent reviews of the literature surrounding governance and performance, Lynn, Heinrich, and Hill (1999, 2000, 2001) assert that consensus on the logic of governance has emerged and can be expressed with the function: $O = (E, C, T, S, M)$, where $O =$ individual-level and/or organization-level outputs or outcomes, $E =$ environmental contingencies, $C =$ client characteristics, $T =$ primary work or core processes or technology, $S =$ structures, and $M =$ managerial roles and actions. They acknowledge, however, that the simple appearance of this function belies the complex set of causal relationships and interdependencies likely to exist among these variables.

stituent components and identifying the dominant relationships between essential elements—a process we have referred to in our earlier work as "dissecting the black box" (Ingraham and Kneedler, 2000a). We initiated this process in 1997 by proposing a preliminary model of government management performance. This model has evolved as our work has progressed.* In this chapter we present the conceptual framework that has developed and guided our analysis of government management. This framework is presented, not as a representation of causal linkages to be tested formally, but as a tool to clarify our assumptions about the placement and operation of management in the government performance system.

The Government Performance Framework

The traditional policy performance equation that relates resources and results through the so-called black box of public management is shown in Figure 2.1. Our work rests on the assumption that if the middle of this equation (public management) operates poorly, then the linkage between public resources and policy results is attenuated, and desired policy results cannot be achieved as effectively as they could be if public management systems functioned well. In short, we assume that well-managed governments and agencies have the ability to perform better than governments and agencies that are less well managed, all else being equal. We therefore assert that better specifying the intervening management variable ultimately allows us to understand the potential and ability of a government to achieve policy outcomes. Given that public organizational systems and managerial activities are drivers of policy outcomes that public administrators control to a large extent, understanding them in detail allows us to get at the heart of government effectiveness.

We propose a conceptual framework that characterizes the key relationships inherent in the government management and policy performance

---

*We first presented our theoretical framework for examining government management at the Fourth National Public Management Research Conference in November 1997. This early model appears in Ingraham and Kneedler (2000a). A further developed conceptualization of government management appears in Ingraham and Kneedler (2000b). Our theory development has benefited greatly from the thoughtful comments of Carolyn Heinrich, Kenneth Meier, and Laurence O'Toole. The analytical rationale presented here also serves as the nucleus for papers related to our research on government management capacity, and the model and explanation in this chapter appear in part in those publications.

Figure 2.1. The classical policy/performance equation

system. Our framework, portrayed in Figure 2.2, enhances the classical representation in which public resources are mysteriously transformed into policy results (Fig. 2.1) by elaborating on the nature and role of government. In our model, policy results emerge from government performance but are also contingent on the environment. Government performance, in turn, is a function of management capacity as well as of an array of environmental constraints and opportunities.*

By *capacity,* we mean government's intrinsic ability to marshal, develop, direct, and control its financial, human, physical, and information resources (Meier, 1988; Meier and Kleiman, 1995; Meier and McFarlane, 1995; Malysa, 1996; Gargan, 1968; Honadle, 1981).† In essence, management capacity concerns the extent to which a government has the right resources in the right place at the right time. Capacity therefore rests on the quality of managers and systems: governments and agencies with strong managers and sound management systems can be described as having high capacity and are more likely to perform better; those with weak managers and shaky management systems have low capacity and are less likely to perform well. A government's capacity is driven by four key levers: the character of the government's management systems, the level and nature of leadership emphasis, the degree of integration and alignment across its management systems, and the extent to which it manages for results.

*The notion that the governance environment presents shocks and opportunities with which management must contend is developed by O'Toole and Meier (1999).
†Our use of the concept of "capacity" both varies from and overlaps with uses of the term elsewhere in public administration and political science scholarship. As many authors have pointed out, a wide range of definitions of capacity appear in the literature, but there is some agreement that capacity is a dimensional concept. Malysa (1996), in fact, provides a useful summary of these definitions and dimensions in the context of state wetlands management. In this research, however, we focus on capacity as it applies narrowly in the context of public management of those functions common across governments. This builds on the work of Meier which relates bureaucratic capacity to government performance and develops a theoretical argument that bureaucratic capacity is necessary for good public policy.

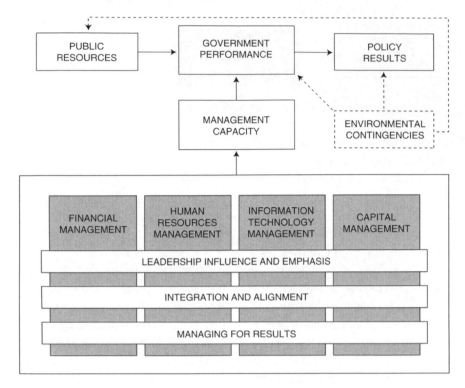

Figure 2.2. The components of public management

The First Lever: Management Systems

In our view, a government's management capacity is fundamentally dependent on the nature of its administrative infrastructure and technology as manifested by the four core management systems identified in Chapter 1: financial management, human resources management, information technology management, and capital management. For most governments, agencies, and policy areas, these systems are likely to be present and are essential both to the quality of management and ultimately to a government's ability to successfully pursue and support public policy goals. The common responsibilities and tasks of the management systems are summarized in Figure 2.3.

These systems were identified on the basis of preliminary analyses during the pilot year of the GPP, which was devoted to determining what management systems and processes comprise government management. We found widespread agreement in the field and the literature—as demonstrated by the tables of contents of innumerable mainstream public administration texts—

that all governments and their agencies perform several core administrative functions. In academic circles, this perspective undoubtedly emerged from the work of Weber (1946) and Taylor (1911) and most prominently from Gulick's classic POSDCORB typology (1937), but it also reflects more contemporary thought. For example, Rosenbloom (1989), in his discussion of the practice of public administration, devotes significant attention to the core functions of budgeting and human resources management and also notes the important distinction financial mangers make between capital and operational budgets. Cohen and Eimicke (1995) additionally include gathering, organizing, and using information as a key managerial tool in the public sector. As explained in Chapter 4, the pilot process also relied on expert advisors—both academic and practitioner—to define key management systems and to identify the qualities that constitute effective systems and processes. Based on our review and these discussions, we believe that the nature of government management rests both on the character of each system—their configuration, tasks, procedures, and work processes—and on the ways in which these management systems are interrelated.

The Second Lever: Leadership

In constructing our analytical framework, we make the assumption that sound leadership has a positive influence on effective management and thus on overall government performance. Here we draw implicitly on the broad existing literature for the scope and definition of this component of government management, though characterizing leadership and its impact on the quality of a government's management is a complex challenge not yet resolved in the literature. One reason the role of leadership is difficult to specify is that the influences of leaders on the behavior of public organizations and institutions are ubiquitous, multiple, and entangled with other forces. Thus, directly measuring the independent effect of leadership is nigh impossible.*

Nonetheless, we argue that leadership contributes to management effectiveness in two significant ways: it influences each management system independently by setting priorities and emphasizing certain activities; and it marshals these systems to operate as elements of a coherent and cohesive

---

*In addition, Ingraham, Sowa, and Moynihan (2002) note that past analyses of public sector leadership include an array of models of leadership and provide important insights into the attributes and activities of successful individual leaders, but do not yield many generalizable or measurable conclusions that permit pre hoc predictions of leadership effects.

Financial Management. Government financial management systems distribute and manage money for public purposes through processes such as procurement, accounting, cash management, and reporting. Financial management includes both budget allocation and budget execution systems. A financial management system that supports performance must determine the appropriate level of resources, allocate those resources according to strategic priorities, and spend money effectively and accountably. Key components of the effectiveness of the financial management system include the ability to engage in accurate revenue and expenditure forecasting, a long-term focus, the practice of planning for contingencies, awareness of the linkage between cost and performance, and appropriate flexibility (Meyers, 1997).

Human Resources Management. Government activities are typically highly personnel intensive and thus personnel systems are a key element of public institutions. Fundamentally, human resources systems are concerned with recruiting, retaining, motivating, training, and terminating public employees. Key aspects of effectiveness in human resources management systems include: the use of coherent procedures, workforce planning, timely hiring, sufficient professional development programs, and meaningful reward structures and disciplinary actions. An additional consideration when evaluating public human resources systems is the relationship between political appointees and career civil servants within governments; that is, political leadership of the career service. Because increased flexibility in the human resources management process has been a consistent focus of administrative reform, it is also important to consider where in the system and for whom such flexibility occurs.

Figure 2.3. The management systems

administrative framework. In this respect, the notion of "vision" commonly identified in the leadership literature is central because it frames the organization's mission—and the consequent goals and objectives—in concert with individual commitment, organizational capability, and societal values to fulfill a broader purpose (see, for example, Ulrich, Zenger, and Smallwood, 1999).

To sharpen the linkage between leadership and management effectiveness, it is necessary to examine how leaders create systemic, systematic, performance-based operational support for mission. It is this manifestation of leadership to which we give our attention. In essence, we focus on the ability of leaders to make informed decisions; to provide guidance and direction; to develop the institution's mission, vision, and values; to communicate these to all its members; and to coordinate the behavior of all organizational components and systems to behave in a manner consistent with

Information Technology Management. The quality and availability of information is crucial to the ability of managers and policymakers to make decisions and carry out the key functions of resource acquisition and policy implementation. Managing information technology includes the development, maintenance, and use of technological systems to collect, analyze, and communicate data. Especially in public institutions responsible for executing complicated programs and interfacing with large, diverse constituencies, information technology performs both primary and integrative functions. It not only responds to information demands particular to specific programs but also supports the information needs of the other management systems. Key components of the effectiveness of the information technology management system include the timeliness, accuracy, reliability, usefulness, and cost-effectiveness of data and the ability of all personnel to use the information systems.

Capital Management. Capital management involves planning for, maintaining, and disposing of, long-lived resources. This area is particularly salient for state and local governments, where capital spending and stock management demands are typically more frequent than in federal agencies (although many federal agencies have large capital responsibilities). Key components of the effectiveness of the capital management system include: active engagement in long-range planning and prioritization of projects, adequate budgetary resources for infrastructure maintenance and repair, and attention to the relationship between the capital and the operating budget.

institutional and broader public values in order to achieve the stated mission and ultimately to realize the policymakers' intent. These influences are likely to manifest themselves as formal structural or procedural effects within the management systems. But they also arise in the attitudes, beliefs, and values of public employees; appear as adjustments to work processes over time; and surface in the feedback processes leaders employ to judge their progress toward organizational goals.

How well such coherence across the management systems is achieved and how the ability to move constructively toward public goals and objectives is created is dependent on leadership at both political and organizational levels. The "duality of leadership" problem in most public organizations—elected and appointed officials formally lead, but those in the career civil service also have a leadership function (Ingraham, 1995; Ingraham, Thompson, and Eisenberg, 1995)—is thus directly relevant to the analysis of management proposed here. That is, we must recognize that although political leadership provides one critical set of directions, resources, and supports for system creation and maintenance, it generally does not interact specifically or consistently with the management systems we analyze. Leadership of those systems is the responsibility of a different set of leaders: those senior executive, appointed, and career officials located within the organizations. Although successful interaction between these two sets of leaders creates an overall vision for the systems and the governments they support and also drives coherent and well-supported movement toward those objectives, our work focuses on the actions of nonlegislative leaders as executive managers of public organizations.

The Third Lever: Integration and Alignment

We have already alluded to another assumption we make about the nature of government management: Effective management is fundamentally concerned with the extent to which the management systems are orchestrated as part of a unified, cohesive whole with shared values, common goals, and allied objectives; that is, the extent to which they are integrated and aligned. We have explained that management is composed of distinct component systems that have typically been considered as separate functions, a legacy that has flowed from early-twentieth-century public administration prescription. Now we further argue that good management depends not only on the quality of each of these systems independently or as ends in themselves, but particularly on the extent to which these management systems operate according to consistent objectives, are mutually supporting, and are well coordinated. In short, we presume that management systems in combination, not in isolation, are more effective.

We suggest that integration and alignment are primarily accomplished through three key activities: the exercise of leadership, which also has other effects that were discussed above; the use of information; and the strategic allocation of resources. We view the action of information and resources as forces for integration and alignment as follows:

Exercise of Leadership. Leaders can serve an important function as shapers and coordinators in the realm of government management. Here we are concerned with the ability of leaders to cause the structures, work processes, and incentives within and across the government's management systems to function in a way that promotes operational coherence and cohesion throughout the government. Leaders are situated within governments, where they can attain perspective on how the management systems interact; thus, they are in a position to ensure that the systems are mutually enabling

—that each system operates in a way that supports the performance of the others. Moreover, beyond ensuring that the systems work cooperatively, leaders are also able to see that the joint effort of the management systems supports a commonly held vision of the achievement of the government's missions, goals, and objectives.

This notion of leaders as integrators is closely related to the literature about network effectiveness. Some research suggests that this role is more effective if centralized (Provan and Milward, 1995). Other authors explain that network managers located at key points of inter-unit contact assume a multilateral brokerage role that ranges along a continuum of shared power from autocrat to mediator and that serves to facilitate the emergence and persistence of cooperative behavior (Mandell, 1990; O'Toole, 1996). Again, the relevance of this view of strategic leadership and management to coordinating administrative systems across agencies and within governments is clear.

Use of Information. The freedom, consistency, and speed with which managers cause information to flow throughout a government; the attention that managers give data; and the willingness of managers to share knowledge converge to facilitate (or thwart) the extent to which a government's management systems are mutually supporting. Although the information technology management system, a mechanism concerned with the collection and availability of timely and accurate data, supports the transmission and use of information, it is the interaction of government managers with information that can enable the management systems to operate in concert.

Allocation of Resources. The decisions that managers make about how resources will be garnered and distributed across a government, and the activities that facilitate this decision-making process, influence the extent to which the management systems are configured to be mutually supporting. The classic example of such an activity is the budget process whereby elected officials and managers negotiate over how money will be apportioned, which fundamentally affects the collective perception of the government's goals and priorities. Another example is the location of capable human capital throughout the government. Although such processes as recruiting and hiring personnel are the purview of the human resources management system, the presence, behavior, and attitudes of people at key points of intersection among the management systems affects the degree of harmony in the system as a whole.

The Fourth Lever: A Results Focus

Another key factor that influences management effectiveness is the degree to which an explicit system of managing for results is present and in use by the government. Such a system, formally developed as a management system by some governments and agencies, can have an important impact on the quality of the other systems. Managing for results is the dominant mechanism by which leaders identify, collect, and use the performance information necessary to evaluate the institution's success with respect to key objectives, to make decisions, and to direct institutional actions. It comprises a set of tools by which organizational learning processes are formalized and is thus an important management system and a key tool for leaders who seek to improve the ability of the whole management infrastructure to support policy outcomes.

Governments and agencies that are managed for results focus continually on discovering the most efficient and effective ways of achieving their objectives, employing these techniques across all management systems and monitoring agency activity in light of these objectives. Such a results orientation rests on three vital components. The first is the ability to identify clear objectives. The second is a means to assess progress toward those objectives according to accepted criteria or standards, a mechanism often referred to as *performance measurement*. The third is an process for assessing performance continuously over time, often termed *performance monitoring*. Thus, management effectiveness is not only driven by the ability of leaders to focus the government on its missions but also by mechanisms for tracking activities and performance relative to overall objectives.

The Environment

It should be noted explicitly that a variety of environmental factors affect government performance and policy outcomes. These factors are considered exogenous to this model. They embody a broad array of influences, including both properties of the larger context within which the government operates and properties of the government's jurisdiction. Examples of environmental factors likely to be significant include characteristics of the constituent populations and socioeconomic conditions. Most of the implementation literature, for example, recognizes the dramatic impact that local environmental conditions can have on the character of programs and their outcomes and thus on policy performance. It is easy to imagine that environmental factors might affect public management systems as well. Human resources management processes, for example, are likely to be affected by demographic characteristics such as the size and qualifications of the available labor pool. Capital management, in turn, would more likely be affected by other environmental conditions, such as the weather. In short, management is contingent; whether better-managed entities actually perform better than poorly managed entities (in other words, whether the quality of their management is translated into a relative level of results) depends in part (sometimes in large part) on the influence of other determinants of policy outcomes such as the political environment or economic conditions.

It is also important to fully acknowledge the roles that politics and the political environment play in good management and effective policy. The effort to tidy the relationship between politics and management is an old problem for public administration and public management. The politics-administration dichotomy is an obvious—and perhaps the most enduring—example. Yet we continue to need frequent reminders that the interactions of politics and processes of public management are core manifestations of the democratic setting in which public management and performance occur (Rosenbloom, 1993, 2001; Lynn, 2001). The political environment plays a crucial role in determining how effective performance will be defined, how public management systems will be structured, and how many resources will be available for translation through those systems (Peters, 1989). For better or for worse, the political setting will be the final judge of good management and of effective performance as well. Our point, then, is not that politics is either a good or a bad influence on management and on the performance equation that we examine. That issue has been extensively, if not decisively, argued elsewhere. Our point is that politics and the political environment are necessary parts of any discussion of efficiency, performance, and management in the public sector.

Units of Analysis

We have presented our model in general terms, implying that it can apply equally well to any level of government—national, state, or local. In fact, our empirical work considers each of these levels, focusing in particular on the quality of the management systems in the government at hand. At the state and local levels of government, we look at the central government as a whole, where these systems predominantly reside. At the national level, individual agencies each have their own set of management systems that are distinct and often dramatically different from parallel systems in other agencies. In our national-level analysis, therefore, we look at individual agencies rather than across the government as a whole.*

The Management-Performance Link

In order to assess an entity's ability to manage, we must understand the relationships among the capacity levers we have just described. Presuming that administrative structures and technologies may be more or less coherent across governments and agencies, that leaders may be more or less effectual, and that the degree to which integration and a managing for results focus exist may also fluctuate, it is possible to imagine that a government's or an agency's ability to manage effectively varies dramatically.

It is conceivable, for example, that a government has the fundamental management systems in place but lacks (or at least fails to communicate) an overarching structure of goals and objectives to unify these systems. Integrative activities such as exercise of leadership focused on the "big picture," sharing and use of pertinent information about the system as a whole, and distribution of resources to support the larger system rather than each individual system are absent. The result is a classic "stove-piped" arrangement, where each management system operates in isolation—and perhaps competition—and has an independent impact on management capacity.

Similarly, it might be the case in a given government that a formalized results orientation is missing, and thus the government has no institutional mechanism for ensuring that the activities of each of the management systems are informed by their impacts on performance outcomes. Absent a coherent managing for results system, cohesion may exist in a government, but it is not driven or enlightened by a perspective of effects, results, and outcomes.

We can guess at the implications such conditions may have for management capacity. In the case where a government is both integrated and supported by an operational managing for results system, the management systems collectively influence the quality of management, and there is an interactive relationship between the management systems and the managing for results system. The vehicle for this interaction is the same set of forces that serves to integrate the management systems. In other words, the exercise of leadership, the use of information, and the allocation of resources all serve

---

*In our analysis, we consider federal agencies to be a significant operating unit of the federal government. We do not limit ourselves to cabinet-level departments.

to bind the tools of performance management to administrative functions. In high-performing governmental entities, the management systems that we identify will most likely contribute powerfully and positively to overall management effectiveness through the intrinsic ability of each to link to, and integrate with, the others. Moreover, each management system, separately and as part of a collective management system, acts primarily in response to the potential for success created by a managing for results perspective and system, which powerfully enhances their overall management capacity. The managing for results system, moreover, is not an isolated function, but one that substantively interacts with the management systems via activities surrounding leadership, information, and resources.

On the other hand, it may be that those governments and agencies in which the management systems operate in isolation from each other and in which performance information is not part of the management process will typically perform relatively poorly. Some likely constraints on performance are that the management systems may work at cross-purposes to one another; success may be inconsistent because it is based upon happenstance rather than systematic feedback; failures may be repeated because there is no mechanism to recognize or institutionalize learning from errors; and organizations may become rule-bound and inflexible in the face of the uncertainty that can arise out of limited information, narrowly focused leadership, and competition for resources.

Why might we hypothesize that the combination of integration and managing for results has such positive effects on the quality of management not seen in their absence? We believe the key is that these two characteristics, acting in concert, lend the government two valuable attributes. The first is the ability to gain and sustain momentum, or the impetus to improve over time. That is, these governments and agencies are particularly good at understanding their progress. Through managing for results they can learn from both successes and failure and can incorporate appropriate support or changes government-wide through integrative mechanisms. The second attribute is the ability to strike crucial balances. For example, these governments and agencies are able to support centralized goals through unifying integrative activities and to simultaneously promote flexibility and innovation through performance-based feedback.

It could also be that either integrative activities or managing for results, but not both, are in place in a government. Our suspicion is that these governments and agencies are likely to underperform because they gain neither the power of one of the two factors nor the synergistic affect of both factors together. Thus, if they seek to achieve good performance, these governments and agencies are likely to have to expend significant energy to overcome their handicap and may develop sophisticated compensation mechanisms that may be recognizable. For example, excessive regulations could compensate for the uncertainty that arises in the absence of performance data, or rigid hierarchies may compensate for poor communication across management systems. Nonetheless, these governments and agencies are likely to derive some positive benefit in terms of performance from the dimension that *is* operating (either integration or managing for results), despite the constraint posed by the absence of the other.

Conclusion

Discussions about the nature of performance and reform efforts aimed at improved performance are integral to contemporary debates about the continuing role of government in society; thus, rigorous analysis of, and prescriptions to improve, government performance must also consider the thorny issue of how to assess and improve government management. In addition, the diversity of interest in public policy and public management suggest the need for an analytical framework that is at once general and parsimonious. That is, to be able to accommodate the multitude of purposes to which it is likely to be put, a model of government management must elegantly capture a complex web of relationships but must also permit variation to be identified along specific, meaningful dimensions. This is the challenge we have begun to address in this chapter.

"A sophisticated understanding of organizational capacity and its subtle influences on policy implementation would require descriptions of virtually the whole gamut of administration, from financial management to motivation, from information systems to affirmative action plans and their impact on the workplace," say Goggin, Bowman, Lester, and O'Toole (1990:120). The conceptual framework we have presented begins to answer this call. Substantively, our model can lend realistic detail to classical input-output models of bureaucracy by disclosing the complexity of management and its influence on organizational effectiveness. It can demonstrate the contribution of management capacity to the ability of government to fulfill its policy promises. It tackles head-on one of the most troublesome and enduring dilemmas of public management research—the issue of the character, role, and impact of government management.

Methodologically, this model calls for cross-system, cross-government, and cross-time comparative study. The GPP and FPP accomplish this to a level of detail and breadth never before undertaken and attempt to tap the power of both quantitative and qualitative analysis to draw conclusions that are richly descriptive and broadly revelatory. As a result of this effort, we are able to evaluate a government's management by assessing it according to the four dimensions we identify: its leadership, its management systems, the degree of its integration, and the character of its results-based management. To facilitate this assessment, it is necessary to specify a system of metrics that permits us to characterize each government along these dimensions. The next chapter develops such a system and discusses its application.

3 | Assessing Management

In Chapter 1 we explained that the bedrock of our work is an important issue for public management researchers, government practitioners, and the citizen-consumers of public goods and services: how to assess management. In Chapter 2, we presented a model that describes the government performance system and identified a set of management systems and dimensions to be evaluated. In this chapter we describe the evaluative system that we have used in this study to support our analysis, facilitate communication about the nature and results of government management systems to citizens, and assist public managers in understanding and learning about successful management practices. In short, we present criteria by which the ability of public entities to acquire, sustain, maintain, and deploy an effective administrative infrastructure can be assessed.

Criteria-Based Assessment

Assessment can be absolute, involving measurement of magnitude, given an arbitrary scale, or it can be relative, involving comparison either against other subjects or against a chosen standard. Of these options, we argue that an example of the second, criteria-based assessment, can be especially fruitful for study of government management. While this technique both offers substantial advantages and poses several challenges, we have found it to be a useful and appropriate approach because it explicitly focuses data collection and analysis efforts around stated beliefs about the nature of good government management.

Advantages

Since the dominant impetus for our research is to explain how public managers can improve government, it is imperative that we be able to define what constitutes good management. It is vital to recognize, however, that we advocate using criteria that describe the positive end-states of sound management activities, not simple prescriptions for behavior. That is, we seek criteria about management quality and effectiveness, recognizing that any of a wide array of managerial tactics may be successfully applied to achieve high performance levels. For example, we might include a criterion that states, "The government has appropriate control over operations and permits sufficient managerial flexibility," as opposed to one that states, "Managers should steer more and row less."

In addition to its explicit focus on standards that define aspects of high-quality management, criteria-based assessment offers the benefit that both the level of a government's management effectiveness and the contributions to its effectiveness can be assessed. That is, by developing and applying a scheme of criteria that represents the desired characteristics of an array of management areas and various functions and activities within these areas, analysts can identify the particular strengths and weaknesses of a government's management systems and the degree to which these affect the government's overall ability to manage. Moreover, the more detailed and sophisticated the scheme of criteria, the more information it can yield. Thus, we believe rating governments against a well-developed set of criteria has the potential to generate more informative analytical results than either an absolute scale, which makes no comment about what is good or bad, or a scale that ranks governments against one another, which emphasizes who performs better than whom rather than who performs well or poorly and why.

Another important advantage to using criteria-based assessment is that this approach facilitates communication of results in two important ways. First, this sort of rating scheme is akin to familiar grading systems, which makes it easily understandable by a variety of audiences, whether or not they are familiar with the statistical or analytical techniques that may underlie the reported assessment results. Second, the use of criteria forces assertions about the desired outcomes of management systems to be explicit, rather than burying them in jargon about the technical aspects of management or obscuring them with prescriptive claims about managerial behavior. In short, criteria-based ratings provide a common language through which meaningful information about a government's management quality and effectiveness can be translated unambiguously amongst citizens, public managers, and researchers.

Challenges

Despite its advantages, criteria-based assessment poses some important dilemmas that must be addressed. An important challenge is choosing a coherent structure for the system. Here the most significant concern is how to weight the criteria. That is, a well-managed government depends unevenly on the outcomes of its management systems. It may, for example, be less consequential that the government produces financial reports in a timely manner than that its budget is structurally balanced, though both factors contribute to the quality of government management. Moreover, the appropriate criteria weights may vary across governments or their agencies. For example, it may be very important for one agency that owns a large number of buildings to have sound capital plans, but this may be relatively trivial for an agency that owns only a few buildings. In short, ratings of a government's or an agency's management ought to account not only for the entity's managerial strengths and weaknesses but also for the relative impact or importance of these strengths and weaknesses for overall effectiveness.

Another significant issue is that this approach fails to control for the influence of environmental factors on managerial outcomes. That is, all governments under study are rated against the same criteria on the basis of their management activities and absolute quality despite the fact that some may face relatively benign managerial environments, while others may face harsher circumstances. For example, consider a case where governments are rated according to a criterion that states, "The government is able to maintain an appropriately skilled workforce." Some governments may be located in areas where the available labor pool is relatively well educated and where many educational institutions operate, whereas others may face a relatively poorly educated population that does not have good access to educational and training programs. The former governments would clearly have an easier time maintaining a skilled workforce than the latter, but under criteria-based assessment, both would be judged in terms of the managerial outcome. Quite possibly the former government would achieve a better result (and therefore a higher rating) than the latter, though it expended much less effort.

The bottom line is that criteria-based assessment emphasizes the nature of managerial activities; it does not give "credit" for effort expended by governments simply to overcome external obstacles to performance. The criteria we have chosen are consciously focused internally on the government rather than outwardly on the environment. This may be viewed as an advantage in the sense that ultimately citizens probably do not care as much about how hard governments work as about what they actually achieve. To the extent that criteria-based ratings reveal managerial end-results, these ratings therefore succeed. On the other hand, under such a scheme, a government operating under difficult circumstances may be taking actions that would, under more favorable conditions, actually result in a higher capacity rating. Conversely, a government may not be performing up to its potential because the relaxed environment it experiences does not exert pressure on it to perform as well as possible. In short, failure to account for environmental disparities risks misrepresentation of the degree to which a government achieves its full potential in terms of management effectiveness. This is an important consideration from several perspectives. For example, citizens may be more forgiving of a government that it believes to be doing the best it can and may be more forthcoming with their tax dollars when confronted with evidence that they will be spent wisely.

Strategies for addressing these concerns are conceivable. It might, for example, be possible to develop a set of environmental criteria to be applied in conjunction with the criteria focused on the management subsystems. Ratings on these criteria could then be used to weight the management capacity ratings. On the other hand, it may be more fruitful to retain ratings that do not account for the environment but to accompany them with careful explanations that include discussion of possible environmental constraints. This is the technique we have employed in our analysis for two main reasons. First, simple (rather than weighted) application of the criteria enhances the transparency of the rating process, and accompanying discussions of environmental constraints can help explain these findings. Second, the sheer variability and intricacy of environmental conditions and the complex ways managers interact with them make development of a defensible weighting scheme that is appropriate to all governments and contexts a formidable theoretical challenge. This is certainly an important puzzle for future work to untangle, given the lessons learned from the present effort.

Defining the Criteria

A final prerequisite to employing a criteria-based assessment approach is specification of appropriate criteria. This requirement posed special challenges in our research because the state of knowledge about each of the dimensions of management described in Chapter 2 is not sufficiently developed to be able to lift an appropriate set of criteria "off the shelf." Moreover, we were wary of conventional wisdom, which can be misguided in any field and which is ambiguous in the field of public management, where very little systematic evidence about the influences on performance has been gathered. Moreover, the interested parties who would make use of an assessment of government management are likely to differ in what they consider to be the most important quality determinants. A policy analyst would probably come up with a different set of criteria by which to judge government management than would a citizen. Furthermore, while national, state, and local governments share much in common with respect to the exigencies of public management, they also vary in ways that require criteria tailored to their unique responsibilities, structures, and circumstances.

As explained more fully in the next chapter, we have addressed these concerns pragmatically. At the beginning of the Government Performance Project (GPP), we consulted a number of sources, including the academic literature (extensive for some areas of management) and previous efforts to evaluate management (such as the Baldrige criteria) to discover what management quality criteria had already been developed. We also convened a group of experts from academe, government, and private business who were considered to be subject-matter experts for each of the management dimensions and systems (financial, capital, human resources, and information technology management, as well as executive leadership and performance management) and asked them what they considered to be the most significant elements of management in their areas. We discovered a high degree of consensus in the literature and among our consultants about what mattered most to successful government management, and we converted these findings into an initial set of evaluation criteria.

Our understanding of management grew as the GPP and FPP progressed. We therefore honed our assessment criteria over the course of the projects. We convened sets of managers at annual learning conferences to reflect on, among other things, whether the assessment criteria had the right focus and substance. We used this feedback, coupled with our growing experience of the efficacy of the criteria in revealing the nature of management practices, to revise the criteria. Thus, the criteria we used evolved, and they were identical neither across levels of government nor across years. It is important to emphasize, however, that the criteria were consistently applied across all entities under study in a given year and at a particular level of government. Also, most were retained over the life of the project with only small fine-tuning modifications.

Evaluating Management Systems

For the remainder of this chapter, we will discuss the substance of, and justification for, the criteria we have chosen, outlining the important dimensions of performance in each management area. Some dimensions apply more appropriately to state and local governments; others are more apt for federal agencies. To clarify the definition and application of criteria in our analysis, we have listed the specific criteria used to evaluate each level of government in Appendixes 3.1–3.3. Even after several years of careful attention and development, we are quite aware that the criteria we have developed and applied are not the only ones that could be used in evaluating management performance. But we are confident that, though any single reviewer may approve of some and disapprove of others or might apply them differently, each of our criteria would receive a great deal of support. Moreover, it is consensus about the framework for analysis that is most important—and to the extent that our propositions spark debate about the specific content of assessment criteria, we view that as a productive contribution to the enterprise of the study of public management.

Financial Management

Government budgeting and financial management systems allocate and administer fiscal resources for public purposes according to professional norms that have developed in the field. The most comprehensive single listing of financial management norms is that offered by Roy Meyers (1997). While several of his principles are outside the scope of an evaluation of management performance (for example, Meyers believes that budgets should be responsive to the needs of citizens and should place decisions in the hands of legitimate authorities), many of his standards fit nicely into a diagnosis of financial management. In addition, in 1997 the National Commission on State and Local Budgeting issued a set of draft recommendations intended to guide budgetary practice. These guidelines focused on a set of activities—a checklist, really—that state and local governments should engage in if they are to budget effectively. We have drawn from these sources in defining our financial management evaluation criteria.

Public finance researchers and practitioners share the fundamental belief that a financial management system that supports a well-performing public sector must allocate resources in line with strategic priorities and have a means of effectively and accountably spending that money. These missions require the dual functions of what budgeting and financial management scholars refer to as budget *allocation* and budget *execution.*

Allocation. Budget allocation questions have dominated the budgeting literature for the better part of this century. In particular, debates among budgeting scholars have focused on whether it is possible to make the budget allocation process more rational. For example, while political scientist V. O. Key (1940) decried the "lack of a budgetary theory" (that is, the absence of a coherent rule to guide the allocation of resources) in the early 1940s, others (most notably Aaron Wildavsky) cautioned that such a rule was unlikely to develop, since the allocation of monetary resources in a democracy is ultimately a political question (Wildavsky, 2001).

Although allocation decisions are made regularly according to annual or biennial processes, governments and agencies must always consider more than just the current fiscal period, and they also need to understand the effects of their actions on others. In effect, budgeting is in large part about predicting future fiscal and policy circumstances. For this reason, the ability of a government to engage in accurate revenue and expenditure forecasting is viewed as important to ensuring that program managers and other recipients of government funds have predictable funding flows (Bretschneider and Gorr, 1987) and that citizens are not overtaxed relative to the services they receive.* In addition, the failure to adopt budgets before the beginning of a fiscal period (year or biennium) creates uncertainty for program managers and others dependent on funds. All else being equal, the later the budget, the worse the situation for managers. The National Commission on State and Local Budgeting (1997) has several practices that relate to compliance with an annual calendar, and R. Meyers (1997) also discusses this as an important practice.

Financial management is likewise a long-term, rather than annual or biennial, proposition. For example, it is worrisome if a government uses nonrecurring revenues to finance continuing expenditures because this can mean that the government will find it more difficult to manage its finances in subsequent years. In its 1997 report, the National Commission recommended that governments "isolate non-recurring revenues" and that they should "develop policies on use of one-time revenues" because "by definition, one-time revenues cannot be relied on in future budget periods." Even with good attempts at foresight, though, all governments are vulnerable to the cycles of the economy, and there will be times when current revenues do not match current expenditure needs. As a result, there is general agreement that a well-managed government puts funds aside as a cushion against unanticipated shifts in the economy.†

---

*In 1997 The National Commission on State and Local Budgeting recommended that revenue forecasts extend over of period of three years or more and that they should "strive for accuracy by coming as close as possible to the actual outcome." See also Rodgers and Joyce (1996).

†While there is general agreement on the desirability of these funds, there is not consensus on the level of the fund, with estimates ranging from 5 percent to more than 30 percent of general fund revenues. Sobel and Holcombe (1996) estimated that states would have

Beyond economic changes, governments and agencies often confront changing service demands and policy priorities. Many are unable to respond to these contingencies because their resource allocation systems favor the status quo.* If a government or agency can determine its policy priorities but cannot align resources in pursuit of those priorities because its budget system is immobile, its ability to achieve its goals will be compromised. A key function of management is therefore to inform budget choices by providing relevant performance information to leaders at key decision points. Moreover, an important impetus behind the move toward performance-based budgeting is the belief that there should be a direct relationship between an entity's policy objectives and its budget (Joyce, 1999). Thus, one area of financial management where many assert that reforms are necessary is expenditure control systems that are viewed as excessively oriented toward control at the expense of performance (Forsythe, 1993; NPR, 1993a).

Execution. Budgets are only meaningful if they represent a real constraint. For this reason, it is important that any budgeting system include "mechanisms for budgetary compliance," or a set of accepted practices for managing money (National Commission, 1997). This can be taken too far. One of the major criticisms leveled against financial management systems by managers is their emphasis on detailed input controls, which are sometimes counterproductive to the flexibility needed to pursue the goals and objectives of the agency. This has led to a general trend in many countries that favors holding managers accountable for results but providing them with additional flexibility in the use of resources to achieve those results (Holmes and Shand, 1995). The tradeoff between flexibility and control, however, is a tricky one, and flexibility that is not coupled with accountability is an invitation to abuse. The development of budget execution activities thus has largely involved the search for better techniques to manage money and ensure predictable financing flows, including how to address issues of spending accountability, cash management, borrowing, and cost accounting, each of which will be discussed briefly.

---

needed a 30 percent rainy day fund in the last recession in order to avoid tax increases or spending cuts. The frequently cited benchmark, established in the late 1980s by the National Conference of State Legislatures, is 5 percent. In all probability, a given state or locality will find that the necessary balance depends on many factors, not the least of which is the degree of volatility in the entity's budget environment (Joyce, 2001).

*Aaron Wildavsky (1964) most notably described the importance of the "base" in budgeting and the recognition that the budget tends to focus on "incremental" changes at the margin.

Spending accountability is accomplished through the application of accepted accounting principles, which have been the focus of a great deal of attention both in the federal government through the Federal Accounting Standards Advisory Board and the Chief Financial Officers' (CFO) Act of 1990 (Jones, 1993; Steinberg, 1996) and in state and local governments through the efforts of the Governmental Accounting Standards Board (GASB) (Harris, 1995). One indicator of sound accounting is that governments are able to produce financial statements that can be independently audited. At the federal level, the passage of the CFO Act and the important role of inspectors general and the General Accounting Office have drawn increased attention to the preparation of accurate financial statements (Jones, 1993). At the state and local level, GASB has taken the lead in issuing guidelines for the preparation of comprehensive annual financial reports (CAFRs) by state and local governments. Standard and Poor's (1986) specifically lists compliance with generally accepted accounting principles (GAAP), which GASB has insisted on, as an important factor in debt ratings.

Another important accountability indicator is competent and comprehensive reporting—it is important that a government or agency be able to communicate financial information in a manner that is understandable to individuals who have an interest in that entity's policies. This may include, for example, citizen-friendly budget and financial reports. As the National Commission report (1997) noted, the budget is "arguably the single most important document routinely prepared by governments." But the budget is a forward-looking document. Reports that review the actual performance of governments relative to the plan are also important to citizen and employee understanding. The assumption here is that the more accessible and widely disseminated the financial reporting, the greater the incentives for accountability.

Managing cash flows is a second key financial management function. This involves not only short-term investment but also the investment of longer-term portfolios (for example, pension funds). It is crucial, however, that governments manage their investments with an eye toward both maximizing return on and protecting the investment. The well-publicized investment disaster in Orange County, California, illustrates the folly of pursuing the first objective to the exclusion of the second (Jump, 1996). Maintaining policies that promote an appropriate balance between these two objectives, then, is crucial to effective cash management.

A third important budget execution function concerns *debt management*. Most governments borrow substantial amounts of money, normally for the construction of long-term assets such as roads, schools, and prisons. It is essential, however, that governments not take on more debt than they are ultimately able to repay. We need only think of the New York City fiscal crisis of the 1970s and the Washington Public Power Supply crisis of the 1980s* for illustrations of the difficulties of over-borrowing (Gramlich, 1976; Leigland, 1986). Bond rating agencies routinely track the debt practices and capacity of state and local governments who issue debt and use these factors as inputs into decisions concerning the creditworthiness of state and local bonds (Standard and Poor's, 1986). We take our cue from this approach and use debt management practices as an indicator of a government's ability to maintain its fiscal health.

Finally, *cost accounting,* or determining costs by mission or accountability centers, is a key component of budget execution that ultimately supports allocation decisions as well. In order to do this, it is crucial that program costs be measured fully and accurately. Moreover, such cost accounting involves not only a determination of direct costs (for example, the cost of people delivering program services) but also indirect costs (costs associated with budgeting, personnel, computers, etc.) related to that program (Anthony and Young, 1999). Only then is it possible to reasonably compare the results that will accrue from alternate uses of government resources.

Human Resources Management

The success of large-scale, personnel-intensive activities is ineluctably tied to the efficacy of the organization in managing those human resources. Personnel is the largest item of expenditure for many governments and government agencies. Management of the public workforce ultimately involves achieving success in the following areas: determining how to fulfill the government's workforce needs, acquiring the necessary personnel, developing their skills, motivating them to work in support of public ends, rewarding them for this behavior, and imposing remedial strategies to improve the performance of those who fail. We will explain briefly each of these key human resources management functions and its relationship to government performance.

It is axiomatic that government performance means having the right people to do the appropriate jobs at the appropriate time. This does not happen by accident. Successful governments and agencies actively plan for a future workforce that meets the needs of the government with respect to

---

*In 1984 WPPS defaulted on $2.25 billion in outstanding revenue bonds.

accomplishing the tasks that are required to achieve government objectives both in the short term and the long term. This involves both determining what personnel are required and devising proper compensation schemes for work performed. This is not a new concern. A 1978 textbook on government personnel management devotes an entire chapter to human resources planning, noting that it is the fundamental "supply and demand" function of personnel management (Shafritz et al., 1978).

Once a government knows what human capital it needs, it must be able to recruit and retain appropriate talented individuals to fill government positions. Knowing which employees to hire is only half the battle. It is also crucial to be able to hire them in a timely fashion. The inability to fill positions when and as needed (whether because of excessive rules, managerial inaction, or some other cause) is a major constraint on effective management. For this reason, the natural follow-on to workforce planning is timely hiring (Shafritz et al., 1978), but it is well known that there are substantial constraints to timely hiring in the public sector, including inability to compete with private sector salaries and benefits, and procedural hoops that add steps (and time) to the process (Hays, 1998).

Although hiring the right people is crucial to performance, it is also vital that the agency be able to maintain the appropriate mix of skills among its employees. This can occur in at least two ways: by having a strategy in place that is designed to retain the employees that most contribute to the agency's performance, and by appropriately training employees to be able to do their assigned jobs, consistent with the mission and goals of the agency or government. Investing in employee development and focusing on employees as assets that require investment are crucial to the achievement of any organization's long-term goals (Van Wart, 1998). Moreover, it is important for governments to recognize that the skills their employees need change as the demands on government change, so ongoing development programs yield better capacity than do one-time training events.

Skilled employees are not valuable to government unless they perform well. Thus, the ability to motivate employees to do their best work in pursuit of the organization's goals is also a key determinant of performance. Motivating employees to do a good job also implies an ability to appropriately reward employees for performance. Rewards may include financial incentives such as bonuses or merit pay, but they also encompass nonmonetary rewards such as additional job flexibility and recognition. These nonfinancial rewards fall under the heading of quality of working life (QWL) initiatives, which attempt to motivate employees by making work more rewarding and reducing employee anxieties (Halachmi and van der Krogt, 1998). Finally, compensation, including both pay and fringe benefits, is also crucial to motivation. Governments are frequently cited as lagging behind private sector counterparts in pay and benefits, causing motivation and morale problems (Siegel, 1998).

Just as rewarding employees who do well is necessary for effective management, so is the ability to discipline workers whose performance is subpar. Sanctions might be financial but might also include additional workplace controls and the ability to terminate employees as appropriate. Frequently, governments and government agencies reportedly find it difficult to discipline and terminate poor performers because bureaucratic and contractual barriers to discipline and termination discourage attempts to do so except in the most severe cases.

Ultimately, developing performance information on human resources management involves devising measures of success in at least the five areas we have discussed. There is, however, less than uniform agreement on what constitutes best practice in many of these areas. For example, discussion of classification and recruitment in government has triggered disagreements between those who believe that it is necessary to place large numbers of political appointees at the top of the bureaucracy to achieve political responsiveness and those who believe that the trend toward more political appointees has impeded effective management of the public sector (Ingraham, 1995).

There are, however, some widespread concerns that have generated calls for reform in recent years, not only in the United States but in many other countries as well. First, there is a clear trend toward simplification of personnel rules and procedures, as occurred in the United States with the obsolescence of the much-vilified SF-171 as a required application form for federal employment (Kettl, 1995). Second, international reforms have included as a key component increased flexibility for managers in hiring and firing and in tailoring jobs to work required, in addition to relaxing many *ex ante* personnel rules. Thus, the consensus is that in order to contribute effectively to government performance, a human resources management system should not rely on arcane, hard-to-understand rules and regulations. Rather, the rules governing the system should be easy to understand and consistently applied. They should also be reconsidered frequently and updated as appropriate.

An important matter in evaluating the activities of human resources managers is the role of unions. As noted above, in governments or agencies with a significant number of unionized employees, collective bargaining agreements can create constraints on management. Even in these cases, however, efforts to maintain open lines of communication and good relations with unions in general can add to flexibility and act as a positive factor in productivity (by, among other things, improving employee morale and minimizing the probability of work disruptions). One author describes unions and managers as "participants in a mutually reinforcing symbiotic relationship" (Tobias, 1998: 258). When that relationship deteriorates, however, the result can be negative for both union and employer. Unions may find their members dissatisfied with their treatment, while employers spend an increasing amount of time dealing with union concerns, frequently expressed in formal grievances.

Information Technology Management

Technological advances have revolutionized the practice of government as they have revolutionized the rest of society. It is now commonplace for most government employees to have personal computers on their desks that allow them access to information and the ability to communicate with co-workers and the general public. Just the presence of technology is not enough, however—it must be used in ways that improve decision making, accountability, and work processes. Evaluation of effective information technology management in the public sector often is much more complex than in the private sector because the goals that are pursued by governments are so much more complicated, because a long-term view is compromised by legitimate political realities, and because of a clear need for a capacity to interface with external users (Bozeman and Bretschneider, 1986).

An effective information technology management system provides managers and policymakers with the information necessary to carry out the key functions of government. From the standpoint of evaluation, it is most important to focus resolutely on the ultimate purpose of an information system, which is to buttress decision making in support of the ends of government. Too often information technology management is delegated to technical staffs within an agency of government, many of whom are not sensitive to the uses of information but simply to the production of it (McClure, 1997). The key concern, in our view, is not how many computers a government or agency has or how up-to-date its software is, but whether managers are actually able to use the information generated by the system to manage their programs.

As with human resources management, planning is central to capacity and performance. Good governments and agencies need to have a multiyear technology plan in place for the enterprise that supports the larger strategic goals and objectives of the entity. In short, there should be a direct relationship between what the entity is trying to accomplish and the contribution of information technology management to that endeavor. It should also treat information technology as an investment, meaning that "extensive scrutiny of costs, benefits and risks" should be central to decisions to acquire information technology systems (McClure, 1997: 262).

It is important, moreover, that the cost of information technology systems be justified by the benefits that are delivered by the system. This requires a well-considered process for identifying the needs that the system will address and justifying the purchase of the system based on the benefits it will deliver. Examples abound of gaps between costs and benefits in public sector information technology projects, including, but not limited to, the Internal Revenue Service's Tax System Modernization and the Health Care Financing Administration's Medicare Transactions System, which were canceled after billions of dollars in cost, having delivered little or no benefit.

Planning for technology is not an end in and of itself, however. It occurs because users have a need for technology to meet their demands. For this reason, it is essential that the development of applications and the acquisition of technology proceed with the needs of users clearly in mind. For example, information technology plans ought to be developed with the input of stakeholders and should be written in nontechnical language so that technology goals and objectives are meaningful to them. But more than this, it is important that, once a decision has been made to acquire technology to support improvements in the organization, this technology is made available to managers in a timely manner. For example, the need for excessive layers of approvals before acquisition can delay the benefits expected from the application of new technology.

A related and important contributor to whether an information technology system can make the right information available to the right managers at the right time is how well the system is coordinated. Whether in a government or in a federal agency, it is essential that someone have an enterprise-wide view of technology. This will facilitate the ability of managers to communicate with each other, because systems are more likely to be compatible. This communication should be fostered not only across components of the entity (state agencies, for example) but also across management systems (financial management, human resources management, etc.). A recent example of increased coordination can be found in the federal government, which, through passage of the Information Technology Management Reform Act of 1996 (also known as the Clinger-Cohen Act) implemented a requirement for chief information officers who "have a direct reporting relationship to the agency head and IRM [Information Resources Management] activities as their primary function" (McClure, 1997: 263).

In the same way that it is ineffectual to have computer systems that do not provide useful information, it is also detrimental to management capacity to have computer systems that managers cannot use. Accordingly, a commitment to training is crucial to the effective use of technological resources. Beyond training for managers and other end-users, governments and agencies must be attentive to the need to acquire and maintain the correct skills among information technology support staff. A recent evaluation notes that the federal government has "perpetually outmoded IT skill bases" (McClure, 1997: 258). Such problems can arrest both planning and implementation of technology solutions.

Finally, in establishing criteria for evaluating information technology management systems, it is important to keep in mind that information is not only a resource for government managers but also a resource that can be used by citizens to assess government performance . For this reason, governments and agencies should have technology systems that enable citizens and other interested parties to gain access to public information, resources, and programs.

Capital Management

In the course of performing their core functions, units of government often acquire a substantial stock of long-term physical assets. For states and local governments, this typically involves the construction of facilities such as schools, hospitals, prisons, public utilities, and highways. The federal government typically spends substantial sums building assets like ships, planes, office buildings, prisons, and veterans' hospitals. The manner in which this capital stock is planned and maintained can be an important component of performance. Capital management is a particularly crucial indicator of performance for state and local governments, since these governments almost always have a substantial amount of capital spending and management responsibility.

Long-range planning is paramount here, as it has been in the other management systems we have discussed thus far. Well-managed governments have some established system for determining and prioritizing their long-term capital needs. In turn, these needs should tie directly to the strategic goals of the entity. In the words of one government circular, planning should start with an evaluation of how "existing capital assets are helping . . . to achieve [an entity's] strategic goals and objectives" (OMB, 1996: ii). Good plans look several years into the future, are realistic in terms of likely future funding, and are meaningful. In short, they anticipate when capital needs will occur and plan for the financing of those capital assets. Moreover, the government or agency needs to be able, at the time that decisions are being made on capital purchases, to differentiate good investments from bad ones; for example, many governments use net present value or internal rate of return to identify worthwhile projects (Schwartz, 1996).

Two problems are common in capital planning and management endeavors. The first problem is that capital budget planning too often occurs independent of planning for the operating budget, though the two are integrally related. Facilities must be staffed, and staffing increases or decreases have accompanying implications for the capital budget (Meyers, 1997). A second problem is the frequent tendency to shortchange maintenance of existing facilities in order to acquire more capital assets or to spend more money in the operating budget. This is understandable—capital assets and current operating expenditures have more constituents and are therefore more politically salable—but it is short-sighted. To quote the Office of Management and Budget: "Even the best planned, budgeted and procured asset will fail to adequately deliver to the public unless an adequate O&M plan is . . . properly executed" (OMB, 1996: vi). For this reason, a well-managed government or agency needs to pay attention to maintaining its existing stock of resources (Barrett and Greene, 1995).

Evaluating Managing for Results

One of the central tenets of government reform movements in the United States and other countries is that a well-managed government or agency should be focused on the results that are achieved by government programs and on the most effective ways of achieving those results, rather than only on the amount of money spent or on the processes of government. *Managing for results* is defined as managing in pursuit of policy performance consistent with the mission and aims of the government or agency. We want a government or agency to have clearly identified objectives and to manage with those objectives in mind. Furthermore, we want these objectives to be consistent with the desires of the citizenry, either directly or as expressed by their elected representatives.

In the United States the movement toward managing for results has manifested itself through substantial efforts at both the national and subnational levels. Most assessments of the United States' effort note that state and local governments have made more progress than the federal government (Bavon, 1995). This progress is not uniform, however; some jurisdictions have moved much further than others in this area (Broom and McGuire, 1995). Perhaps the most widespread initiative at the state and local level is the GASB-led drive toward improved Service Efforts and Accomplishments (SEA) reporting. This effort focuses on financial reporting: the GASB urges state and local governments to address, in annual financial reports, not only the expenditure of money but also the use of these resources, including measures of customer satisfaction and comparison to benchmarks of performance (Hatry and Fountain, 1990). In the federal government, the majority of attention has been focused on two initiatives. The first was Vice President Gore's National Performance Review, which advocated a reduction of hierarchical controls over administrative processes in favor of empowering managers and holding them accountable for results (Kamensky, 1996). The second is the Government Performance and Results Act (GPRA), which directs all federal agencies to engage in strategic planning, objective setting, and performance measurement (Joyce, 1993).

Governments that manage for results focus continually on discovering the most effective ways of achieving their objectives, employing these techniques across all management subsystems, and monitoring agency activity in light of these objectives. This means that they must have the ability to identify clearly what their objectives are—what Holmes (1996) refers to as "clarity of task and purpose." Moreover, they must have a means to assess progress toward those objectives (for a detailed discussion of various aspects of performance measurement, see Newcomer, 1997).

In effect, managing for results in government, as in business, starts with knowing where you want to go. Thus, we emphasize the importance of strategic planning as a process that articulates the mission and goals of the organization, and long-term strategies for achieving those goals. Within a government, strategic planning can exist both centrally and at the agency level, but they are considered to be the foundation for an effective system of managing for results (Joyce, 1999). In addition, the process by which the plan is developed may be more important than the existence of the plan itself. Ownership of the plan by key constituency groups is crucial to the maintenance of clear, stable goals and objectives. Thus, such participation is a specific requirement of government efforts such as GPRA (GAO, 1997).

Even if a government or agency knows where it wants to go and has general agreement among important actors about how to get there, it still must be able to appropriately gauge its progress toward meeting its goals. In order for this to occur, the government or agency needs good outcome measures that measure not simply workload or activity but performance in terms of actual policy results (cleaner air, safer streets, healthier people, and so on). Much of the current focus on managing for results has been precisely on the development of appropriate measures (Hatry and Wholey, 1992). Anecdotal evidence shows that most public entities have a great many measures; the problem is that many of these measures enable them to track activities rather than results.

In the end, of course, it is of limited use to a government or agency to know where it is going and to have measures to evaluate its progress without using this performance information for policymaking or management. Use may involve making important macro-level budget or personnel decisions using performance information, or it may involve using performance information to manage resources after they are received. Whatever the use, a mature, well-developed performance measurement system must go beyond simple existence of measures that are focused on the key objectives of the agency. It must involve using those measures as well.*

It is also essential that a government or agency be able to communicate information about success or failure to people who care about the programs it manages. These reports should not be "cleansed" of information that might put the entity in a negative light; it is essential that the reports serve as a transparent accountability mechanism. The advances in information technology that have made so much information available on the internet represent an important mechanism through which this goal may be achieved. To note one example, the state of Missouri includes what it refers to as "Show Me Results" on the state's web site, enabling anyone using the site to access useful information on the performance of Missouri in key policy areas (see www.state.missouri.gov).

We assume that managing for results is one factor that separates the best-managed governments or agencies from those that are performing at a lower level. This is not the same as saying that a given entity could not be well managed in the absence of such a scheme. Many find it quite difficult to manage for results, in part because they lack a clear sense of task and pur-

---

*On the use of performance measures for budgeting, see Joyce (1999). On the use of performance measures in general, see Kettl (1995).

pose. Indeed, in some governmental systems (and perhaps the United States is the best example), the intentional fragmentation of authority promotes this lack of goal clarity. For this reason, we do not assume that managing for results is a necessary prerequisite to good management, but we do assume that it promotes better management.

Evaluating Integration and Alignment

As we noted in Chapter 2, effective management implies that management systems do not simply operate as ends in themselves but function together toward some common and reinforcing purpose. Too often management is "stove-piped"; that is, people speak of financial management or human resources management without understanding that the most important focus should be on how the financial and human resources management systems work together toward some unified set of goals and objectives. The public administration literature is relatively silent on the importance of this kind of integration and completely silent on its specific manifestations. We therefore faced somewhat of a quandary in capturing integration in specific criteria, and we arrived at a solution where our ideas about integration are embedded throughout the criteria that support assessment of each of the management systems discussed above, as a review of the criteria defined in the appendixes for this chapter reveals.

As we explained in Chapter 2, we believe that integration manifests itself in three ways: (1) in the exercise of leadership at the top or center of the organization; (2) in the allocation of resources toward the achievement of some common, specified purpose; and (3) in the use of information, both for day-to-day management and as feedback to policy and program re-design. Indicators of integration in a government or agency can thus be characterized in three ways:

Having a clear mission and vision. A strong leader knows where he or she wants the organization to go, and has a vision for the future that sets the agenda for crosscutting management solutions. A good leader is able to communicate this vision in a manner that is clear and unifies the workforce behind common purposes (Halachmi and van der Krogt, 1998). This is fully consistent with the traditional view of successful public sector managers as effective leaders (Behn, 1991).

Providing the right information to the right people at the right time. Just as the strategic deployment of information is important to judging the performance of the technology system itself, it is also important to the overall management of the government or agency. Decisionmakers and managers must have the data they need to make decisions at the times that are critical to the effective operation of programs and delivery of goods and services. If a manager turns his computer on and nothing happens, the best data in the world will do him or her no good.

Providing the right resources to the right people at the right time. It is not enough to make the resources available that will enable a given government or agency to perform mission-critical work. These resources must get to the people who need them when they can be applied to the problems or situations that enable the entity's goals to be achieved. This suggests that attention must be paid to financial and human resources management systems as "enabling" (providing incentives for) performance, rather than serving as impediments to performance (for example, by imposing an overly rigid set of *ex ante* spending controls) (Holmes and Shand, 1995).

Evaluating Leadership

This chapter has now discussed three of the four factors that were posited in Chapter 2 to be important components of management—administrative structure and technology (the management systems), managing for results, and integration—but not the fourth, leadership. As suggested in Chapter 2, leadership is assumed to operate to affect management in different ways across the organization at different times. We consider leadership at the top to be crucial to effective integration of management in pursuit of established objectives, but we also consider leadership to be an important factor that affects success within each of the management subsystems.

Public sector leadership involves people in positions of authority influencing the direction of the organization, be it a government as a whole or a particular agency within a government. The public sector has three categories of leaders—elected officials (who may reside in either the executive or legislative branches), appointed officials, and career officials (the vast majority of the last two reside in the executive branch) (Abramson, 1989). There is a paucity of research on the impact of leadership on the quality of management at a government-wide or agency-wide level. Research on leadership has tended to focus, rather, on the characteristics of individuals as they manage large-scale processes in pursuit of established objectives.

A continuing feature of leadership studies is their focus on the traits and characteristics of strong leaders that differentiate them from weaker leaders. For example, Abramson (1989) posits that leadership is a function of three factors—vision (an alternative future to the status quo), communication (both internal to the organization and with stakeholders), and hard work. Cohen (1993), in a similar vein, focuses on learning and directing, innovation, and attention to results among many functions of effective public leaders.

For the purpose of developing a model of management performance, however, it is difficult to define the precise criteria to use to evaluate leadership prior to its exercise or demonstration. As noted above, leadership can be exercised at different levels of the organization and for different purposes. Leadership at the center (be it a government or agency) can be different than leadership at the periphery. Leadership for information technology might be exercised in different ways than for financial management. For this reason, while we consider the role of leadership to be central to successful management, we decided against the inclusion of a separate management category called "leadership," preferring instead to embrace the view that leadership (like integration) is developed and exercised in important ways throughout an organization. Put differently, it is our view that leadership can affect (in positive or negative ways) performance on a great many of our criteria; we thus believe that it is most appropriate to constantly evaluate leadership rather than to assume that it is a discrete category of management. In fact, our pilot-year respondents recommended against assessing leadership using a separate group of criteria and survey questions.

Toward a More Comprehensive Approach to Management

If government management is important, then it must be equally important to know how to tell a well-managed government or agency from a poorly managed one. The initial step must be to isolate the key components of management in an effort to focus attention on those areas of management that are most crucial to government performance. But it is also essential to view management as a unified, integrated whole. This book contends that an approach that views management through a holistic lens will focus attention on those areas of management that we assume to be most crucial to the policy performance—safer streets, healthier people, cleaner air—that citizens desire. In this way, management is not a dry, mechanistic enterprise but is crucial to accountability of government to its stakeholders.

The next steps beyond this exercise are to develop the specific methodology that would be necessary in order to test the extent to which a given agency or government is satisfying these criteria, to collect data on the actual practices of these entities, and to evaluate them by comparing their practices and the criteria. The following chapters will make these connections in our effort to develop a more sophisticated understanding of management.

In order to improve management, we have to answer two questions: What is happening now? and What could be done differently? It is our expectation that the development of models, criteria, and a methodology will enable us to make substantial progress in answering these two questions. But given the scarcity of empirical information on effective management practices, perhaps the most important function of our research will be to promote a continuing dialogue among academics, practitioners, journalists, and the public concerning the importance—and the components—of good management in the public sector. In addition, however, there is a practical dimension: those activities that are most inhibiting performance are those that are most worthy of focusing efforts to improve.

4 | Research Methodology

The Government Performance Project (GPP) and the Federal Performance Project (FPP) seek to evaluate the quality of management in states, local governments, and federal agencies. In the previous chapter, we identified a set of criteria that we believe should inform this evaluation. Having these criteria represents only part of the challenge, however. We needed to select entities to study, determine how the criteria would be applied to evaluate public management in these entities, collect data, actually apply the data to the criteria, and reach conclusions concerning the quality of management in these jurisdictions and agencies. Each of these steps required that we make a number of crucial decisions in order to ensure that the results were a valid indicator of the quality of public management.

Selecting the Entities for Study

As a condition of the grant award, the Pew Charitable Trusts required a pilot test of the criteria and methodology using a set of entities representative of those that would eventually be studied and graded. This meant that we needed the agreement and participation of a number of federal agencies, state governments, and local governments. The entire first year of the project was spent in choosing these pilots, evaluating them, and then revising the criteria and methodology based on what we learned during that process. Subsequent to the pilot year, we needed, on an annual basis, to select governments and agencies that would be included in the analysis.

Selection of Pilots

Three criteria were paramount in establishing which jurisdictions and agencies should be selected as pilots. First, it would be most useful to identify pilots who (at least by reputation) were active in thinking about or practicing management reforms or innovations. We consulted various management experts and knowledgeable insiders to determine potential pilots that exhibited this characteristic. Second, because we could not compel them in any way to cooperate with us, they needed to be volunteers, which meant making a commitment to filling out the necessary documents and providing feedback that we could use in revising the process, survey, and methodology.

Third, the pilots needed to be somewhat representative by geography (in the case of states, for example), by mission (in the case of federal agencies), or by type of government (among local governments, we needed cities and counties). We had expected that it might be necessary to contact more than fifteen prospective pilots in order to secure the cooperation of the necessary number, but this was not the case.

The five federal agencies were selected after consultation with officials from the Office of Management and Budget (OMB). It was important that we select agencies that had been actively involved in thinking about management reform or improvement. From this group, an effort was made to identify agencies that were involved with different types of activities—regulatory (the Food and Drug Administration), direct service (the Veterans Health Administration), military (the Defense Logistics Agency), law enforcement (the Coast Guard),* and research and development (the National Aeronautics and Space Administration). Identifying the agencies was the easy part. We also needed to find some way to convince agencies to participate. To that end, we solicited the assistance of the President's Management Council (PMC), which consisted of the deputy secretaries of the major cabinet departments and other federal agencies, and was chaired by the deputy director for management of the OMB. The principal investigator briefed the PMC in the fall of 1997. By October 1997, each agency whose participation was requested had agreed to come on board.

The state and local pilot selection presented different challenges. At the state level, we wanted to select pilots that were politically representative and that also represented different geographic regions, in addition to being leaders in government management and reform. Using contacts from the National Association of State Budget Officers, we contacted officials in five states—Kansas, Arizona, Oregon, Ohio, and Florida—who agreed to serve as pilots. For local governments, we needed to have representatives of the different types (counties and cities), while considering other factors as well. For example, we wanted to identify at least one strong mayor city in addition to council-manager cities. The five local pilots selected included three cities —Phoenix (city manager), Virginia Beach (strong mayor), and Philadelphia (strong mayor)—and two counties—Hennepin County (Minnesota) and Cuyahoga County (Ohio).

---

*The Coast Guard is not a classic law enforcement agency; it occupies a position somewhere between military, regulatory, and law enforcement. Clearly, however, law enforcement is an important part of the agency's mission.

Selection of the Governments and Agencies to Evaluate

Beginning in the spring of 1998 and annually subsequent to that year, project staff faced the task of identifying which entities to evaluate. Early on, the decision was reached that the states and selected federal agencies would go first. The states went first largely because we viewed it as important to evaluate them twice over the three remaining years of the project. Focusing on them in the first (post-pilot) year would permit us to look at them again in the third. There was clearly no "selection" issue for the states—all fifty of them were included in the analysis—but the question of when to do them was a crucial one.

The question of which federal agencies to include occupied more time during the early part of 1998. Two decisions were made that were crucial to federal agency selection, both this year and subsequently. First, the term *agency* was defined as meaning the operating units of the federal government as opposed to (for example) cabinet departments. Cabinet departments are often loosely connected groups of organizations that are only tangentially related to each other. For example, the Treasury Department includes both the Financial Management Service and the Secret Service. The Agriculture Department includes both the Food and Nutrition Service and the Forest Service. Therefore, we decided that we would define *agency* as being a subcabinet entity (that is, the Food and Nutrition Service or the Forest Service, not the Agriculture Department) because this would enable us to focus on agencies in terms of how they chose to manage in order to address their missions. This process is considerably more straightforward at the subcabinet level.

Next, once we had defined *agency* in this way, we needed to have some means of choosing which agencies to include. The narrower definition meant that there were potentially hundreds of agencies that could be chosen for study. Project resources, however, dictated that a much smaller number be done. We decided to study those agencies that had the most direct impact on the public. Many of these choices were easy to make (the Social Security Administration and the Internal Revenue Service, for example); others were more difficult. There was a high correlation in the end between our population of agencies and the thirty-two agencies that made up the National Performance Review's list of "high impact" agencies.*

*The National Performance Review was an initiative undertaken by the Clinton administration in March of 1993 and continuing throughout the Clinton presidency to pursue management improvements in federal agencies. It was later renamed the National Partnership for Reinventing Government.

The final issue was which local governments to include. We were committed to studying both cities and counties over the course of the project, and some consideration was given to looking at both simultaneously. We decided, however, that looking at both of them together would require us to look at too few entities. For this reason, the project focused on cities in year two and on counties in year four.

We clearly could not look at all cities, however. According to the U.S. Census, there are more than nineteen thousand municipalities (the census equivalent of "city") in the United States. These range in size from very small jurisdictions, such as New York or Los Angeles, to tiny governments serving a thousand or fewer citizens. We chose to focus on the largest cities, in large part because these are the cities that have the impact on the most people's lives. Cities were ranked according to the size of their budgets, and the thirty-five largest were ultimately chosen for study. (Project staff judged thirty-five to be the maximum number that could reliably be studied, given the resources available.) We used budget size rather than population because it is a more relevant measure of the importance of the city as a governmental unit. If population were used, for example, there is a chance that we would select a city for study where the city government is a less important actor because many services are provided by the county (or even the state) instead of the city.

In summary, then, the following entities were evaluated over the first four (post-pilot) years of the project:

- Year 1 (1998; publication in 1999)—the 50 states and 15 federal agencies
- Year 2 (1999; publication in 2000)—35 cities and 5 additional federal agencies
- Year 3 (2000; publication in 2001)—the 50 states and 7 additional federal agencies
- Year 4 (2001; publication in 2002)—40 large counties and 6 federal agencies

The specific cities, counties, and federal agencies selected are listed in Appendix 4.1.

Collecting the Data

The criteria used throughout the project were always treated, in a sense, as "works in progress." That is to say, GPP and FPP staff and faculty recognized fully that experience and field learning needed to be consistently integrated into the fine tuning of the criteria. At the outset of the project, there was simply no "cookbook" of generally agreed upon and generally testable propositions. Rather, we were faced with the rather daunting task of having to convert our management criteria into a methodology that would generate useful information that could be used not only to reach general conclusions about the management of these agencies but also to "grade" them in each of the management areas. An important role of the pilot process was to permit us to test a set of assumptions about criteria and methodology in order to develop a greater consensus about what to study.

In addition to selecting the pilots themselves, the pilot process needed to focus on the criteria and methodology. This process began in the pilot year by convening panels of experts (academics and practitioners) in each of the five management areas.* They advised us concerning what criteria to focus on, appropriate survey questions to ask, and how to evaluate responses.

The panels were selected specifically to be representative of both academics and practitioners and to be representative of individuals with both state and local, and federal expertise. For example, the session on financial management included a county budget director, a deputy state budget director, a former federal OMB official, and an academic who had written extensively on developing standards for good budgeting. Other panels were similarly constituted. The six panel discussions were held in Washington, D.C., in early 1997.

These panels operated according to one of two formats, depending on the level of consensus in the academic literature concerning standards for particular management areas. At one end of the continuum, financial management represented an area of substantial consensus concerning standards for success. For example, virtually everyone agrees that a well-managed government accurately forecasts revenues and expenditures, makes use of countercyclical planning devices (such as rainy day funds), and does not balance its budget by using nonrecurring revenues. Human resource management was a source of a roughly equivalent level of consensus, focusing on such issues as workforce planning, appropriate reward and discipline, and matching skills with needed capacities. In these two cases, the panel was given a draft set of criteria and asked to respond to it and to suggest possible ways of collecting data to determine compliance with the criterion.

---

*A sixth meeting was convened to discuss how the project would handle the question of leadership. We decided not to include a separate category for evaluating leadership, since leadership was crucial to building and sustaining management capacity in each of the other five management areas.

Far less consensus existed in other management areas. In these areas, the meetings would begin with a question: "What are the appropriate standards for evaluating . . . ?" (information technology management, for example). We would then attempt to build the criteria and then the methods of collecting data to determine the extent to which agencies are behaving consistent with the criteria. The agenda for these meetings was clearly more challenging than for the former, and project staff viewed the set of criteria and the methodology that emerged from these meetings as more speculative and subject to subsequent revision than the standards for financial management and human resource management. The lack of finality of these standards did not concern us at this stage of the research, since one of the main purposes of the pilot year was to test the criteria and methodology and to get feedback from the pilots concerning their appropriateness. Since the original criteria were established by informed committee procedures, they erred on the side of comprehensiveness and needed to be field tested in order to determine which were the most meaningful and the extent to which any of them were redundant or overlapping.

Upon securing the agreement of the pilots, our first step was to convert the criteria that we had developed into specific survey questions. As noted, our earlier meetings with the various expert advisory groups to identify criteria had also generated a number of specific survey questions in each of the five survey areas. We now solicited other questions from these advisors and from other evaluations of management that had been conducted. For example, we looked to questions underlying the Baldrige criteria used to give the President's Quality Award,* we reviewed evaluations by the U.S. General Accounting Office, and we included some questions that had been part of earlier evaluations published in *Financial World* magazine. In the end, the exploratory nature of the surveys was apparent; they were more than eighty pages long.

Surveys were mailed to the pilots in the spring of 1997, and we gave them approximately six weeks to return their responses. Despite the labor-intensive nature of the survey process, twelve of the fifteen pilots submitted completed surveys. For different reasons, three pilots—one state (Arizona), one local government (Virginia Beach), and one federal agency (NASA)—declined to complete the survey. Staff at the Campbell Institute summarized the survey

*The Presidents' Quality Award, begun in 1988, seeks to recognize federal government organizations that achieve marked improvements in their operations by implementing the tenets of Total Quality Management (TQM).

results and drafted brief reports that were provided to the pilots for their reaction. When we secured the agreement of the pilots to participate, we promised that, in exchange for their assistance, we would treat as confidential the information they provided to us. Thus, no information received from any pilot or evaluations of the pilot were shared with anyone other than that pilot itself.

After the pilot surveys were received and analyzed, we revised the criteria and process based on what we had learned during the pilot phase. The process of gaining feedback from the pilots involved obtaining input from them on an individual basis and also holding a series of meetings designed to get collective feedback from them. Most significantly, two separate "learning" conferences were held with the pilots as a group in order to get general feedback on each of the items discussed above (the criteria, the survey, and the process). The first of these, which focused on the state and local pilots, was held in conjunction with *Governing* magazine's annual conference in September of 1997. The second, covering the federal agencies, was held at United States Coast Guard headquarters in late 1997 and included representatives of each of the federal pilots who completed the survey. In addition, project staff briefed a number of other professional organizations, such as the National Association of State Budget Officers, following the pilot year in an effort to get both substantive feedback and buy-in.

The first notable result of these meetings was the remarkable degree of consensus that the management areas were the correct ones to focus on and that the criteria used were the most appropriate ones for evaluating these entities. One specific outgrowth of the pilot year was some refinement of the criteria for federal agencies so that they began to differ more substantially from the criteria that had been used to evaluate states and localities. Also, the feedback that we got from the governments themselves assisted us in beginning to identify places that the surveys themselves could be cut down or questions clarified.

Second, we began to get both positive and negative feedback concerning the process and methodology anticipated for the future. Some notable examples:

- Universally, the pilots argued that the survey was too long and too cumbersome. They made many specific recommendations on areas of redundancy that could be addressed and on questions that should be eliminated because the cost of answering was not justified by what could be learned by the response. There were also a number of suggestions for additional or reworded questions.

- The state pilots were adamant that the issue of *Governing* that would be devoted to the reporting of the state results not appear until after the November 1998 elections, when more than two-thirds of the states would have gubernatorial elections. They argued that, if the issue appeared before the election, it could lead to all manner of shenanigans because opponents of incumbent governors in states with mediocre or bad grades would be able to use the project results against the incumbent.

- On the other hand, we began to hear from many of the pilots that they had found the process to be a useful learning experience. The Coast Guard, which estimated that it devoted more than six hundred "person-hours" to completing the survey, treated it as an opportunity to get what the agency described as a "penalty-free external assessment." A representative of the state of Oregon suggested that the information included in his state's survey would be useful reading for any Oregon state legislator as an introduction to managing Oregon state government. In short, there seemed a strong probability that pilot participants believed that the project would contribute useful information.

In addition to the specific feedback from the pilots, the project benefited from the advice of a Senior Advisory Board made up of a number of current and past public officials and journalists. This board was chaired by former Senator Mark Hatfield (R-OR), and included as members former Florida Democratic Governor Reubin Askew, Milwaukee Mayor John Norquist, Smithsonian Undersecretary Constance Berry Newman, and former *New York Times* reporter David Bernham. In fact, as a specific condition of the continuation of the grant beyond the pilot phase, this group needed to endorse the concept and methodology of the study. This board met in July of 1997 and made a specific set of recommendations concerning actions they believed needed to be undertaken prior to launching the post-pilot phase of the project. At a subsequent meeting in November 1997, they gave their formal endorsement of the project.

Show Time

Armed with our revised conceptual framework and assessment criteria, we now confronted the issue of how to collect reliable data that meaningfully reflected the nature of government management and that supported conclusions that could be communicated effectively to a wide audience. Two challenges were embedded in the issue of data collection and analysis. The first challenge was that, in both a philosophical and practical sense, our fundamental goal was to understand "the truth" about government management performance, a complex, multi-dimensional phenomenon. Objective data—long considered the gold standard of reliability and validity—can lend insight into the nature of the organizational configurations and activities experienced by governmental actors and stakeholders. At the same time, "truth" or "reality" is arguably relative, suggesting that some combination of perspectives is necessary to capture the richness that comprises the phenomenon of public managerial behavior and therefore that data should be collected about the perceptions of different actors involved in government management.

The second challenge was that, in any data collection effort, the purpose for which any data are to be used influences both the form the data must take and the method by which they are collected. The dilemma we faced in our work is that we sought to fulfill multiple purposes—and satisfy multiple audiences—at once. That is, we sought data that would support a variety of analyses to meet the needs of an array of interested parties (academic researchers, government practitioners, elected officials, citizens, and so forth). Therefore, our data needed to be as rich as possible without sacrificing validity.

To meet this dual challenge of representing reality as closely as possible and of communicating to a variegated audience, we recognized that no single data collection or analytical methodology would be fully satisfactory. We therefore adopted the multimeasure, multiperspective approach advocated by Provan and Milward (1995). Subjective and objective, quantitative and qualitative data about government management systems are collected in the course of our work using a multitude of instruments, including written surveys, interviews, and secondary data from various sources. Accordingly, while the pilot phase had focused primarily on the development of criteria, process, and a management survey, the complete process agreed to after the pilot phase embraced an approach involving multiple methods of collecting data. Project staff, the Senior Advisory Board, and the pilot entities all agreed that such a multidimensional approach was essential to generating valid results. Ultimately, therefore, four main sources of data informed the conclusions reached for the GPP and FPP:

- A management survey, filled out by some centralized source or sources within the government or agency. These surveys were divided into five sections to match the five management categories (managing for results, financial management, human resource management, capital or physical asset management, and information management).

- Documents issued by or about the government or agency, including both internal documents (for example, strategic plans) and external evaluations (for example, audit reports), and follow-up discussions and interviews to clarify the contents and conclusions of these reports where necessary.
- Extensive interviews conducted by reporters from the magazines, which focused primarily (but not exclusively) on individuals and organizations external to the government (or at least the executive) or agency.
- A manager's survey (for the federal portion of the project, only in 2000), which was designed to get a field-level take on management practices and challenges in each federal agency.

The Management Questionnaire

In each year a key initial step was to identify a contact person in each agency or government. This person was to act as the key liaison between the project and the entity being studied. When surveys were mailed out from the university to the state, locality, or agency, the liaison took the lead in deciding who within the government/agency was the appropriate person to respond to each section (or, in some cases, to individual questions within a section).

The survey was mailed out with a specific timetable for return. There was no specific way to enforce adherence to this timetable, and the timing of the receipt of responses varied widely. Throughout the project, a relatively small number of entities actually returned the survey by the deadline indicated. The process typically involved a fair amount of negotiation between the academic institution and the government or agency. Significantly, over the first three years of the project, more than 95 percent of the entities that received the management questionnaire returned it. Many of the respondents provided very thorough responses (the states of Virginia and Washington sent boxes of information, as did the United States Coast Guard, for example). There were also a cases, however, where responses were Spartan or incomplete, and staff at the Maxwell School and The George Washington University spent considerable time and effort working with survey respondents to fill information gaps.

The high response rate for the management questionnaire should not overshadow the reluctance with which some respondents approached the project. Some agencies/governments initially declined to fill out the questionnaire. Most were persuaded by the projects' policy that data would be gathered from other sources were it not forthcoming from the governments themselves. In fact, one of the main purposes of the management questionnaire was to give entities an opportunity to "tell their own story," thus minimizing the chance that we would miss some development or story that the entity itself found significant.

One of the most important functions of the pilot process and the annual feedback received from agencies and governments was to continue to refine the survey instruments. The most important focus of this effort was to narrow the scope and reduce the length of the survey so that only data essential to the analysis of the governments and agencies were collected and so that we could ensure the most effective use of limited resources.

Documents

The second source of information that we accessed included various documents that were considered relevant to the evaluation of management. These can be divided into the following general categories:

Budgetary Information. For states and local governments, the project routinely reviews both executive budget documents and comprehensive annual financial reports (CAFRs). For federal agencies, the project frequently reviewed agency budget justifications prepared for the Congress. These documents were particularly useful in evaluating governments and agencies in financial management.

Strategic Plans and Performance Reports. Particularly for the managing for results area, strategic plans and performance reports were a very useful source of information. At the state and local level, the reports evaluated included both government-wide plans and reports (where available) and selected agency-level reports. For federal agencies, the reports that were prepared as required by the Government Performance and Results Act (GPRA) were particularly useful, but some agencies also had prepared additional reports.

Internal and External Audits. Virtually all governments have internal and external financial audits that present information about spending, revenues, and internal controls. For state and local governments, these are frequently prepared under the supervision of an independent (frequently elected) official. For federal agencies, these may be done by inspectors general (within the agency), by the General Accounting Office (GAO), or by some outside firm. In addition, the GAO and some state and local auditors do program and performance audits, which often present useful information on management practices.

Civil Service Frameworks and Strategic Human Resource Planning Documents. State and local governments varied widely in the nature of their civil service frameworks and reforms and in the nature of their labor/management agreements and environments. Documents describing these policies and procedures were a useful source of information. Workforce planning documents were also useful.

Technology plans. Likewise, many entities had engaged in extensive technology planning, and these documents were sometimes useful in assessing compliance with the projects' information technology criteria. They were only useful to the extent that they presented a clear case for why the acquisition of hardware and software were necessary in terms of the ability of the government or agency to better achieve mission results.

Satisfaction Surveys. Two forms of "satisfaction surveys" were consulted. First, many states, localities, and agencies routinely do surveys of their "customers" in an effort to determine the extent to which these users of government services are satisfied with the services received. These survey results were useful, in particular, in evaluating managing for results. Second, many of the entities under review had done employee satisfaction surveys, which were very useful in determining employee morale and other factors considered in the evaluation of human resource management.

Interviews

Interviews conducted by reporters from each of the magazines were also important sources of data for the project. Reporters did extensive interviews with officials both inside and outside of the entities being reviewed. Heaviest emphasis was placed on interviews with people outside of the agency or government in order to gain an external perspective on the entity being reviewed. Concerns for fairness dictated that the same types of individuals be interviewed for each entity, since it was important that the comparative evaluations not be biased by having interviewed different types of people in different governments or agencies. In addition, all interviews were guided by the criteria for the projects.

As noted earlier, projects such as these, which are simultaneously academic research and journalism, are almost (if not completely) unprecedented. Accordingly, the use of journalistic interviews as a primary source of data for a project that is also a source of academic research is also unprecedented. The goal, in the use of reporters, was to combine the strengths of academics (primarily, in this case, attention to methodology and consistency in research) with the strength of journalists (skill in interviewing and access to established sources of information). This necessitated some "acculturation" of journalists to make them think more like academics. It meant, practically speaking, that the journalists needed to pay attention both to interviewing a consistent set of actors and to asking a consistent set of questions (related to the criteria) in doing their work. This kind of stricture was a new experience for many of the journalists, but it was absolutely essential to ensuring a valid result. That said, however, there were some differences between the state and local process and the federal process that are worth noting.

State and Local Governments. Over the first three years, an average of about one thousand interviews per year were conducted. In every case, key government officials were interviewed, including budget directors, chief personnel officers, and chief technology officials. Legislative representatives were also interviewed in addition to representatives of labor unions, stakeholder groups, media focused on management issues, and representatives of citizen watchdog organizations (as applicable).

Federal Agencies. Over the first three years of the project, more than fifteen hundred interviews were conducted by reporters at *Government Executive*. The interviews involved a number of different reporters, since *Government Executive* decided to make use of its existing reporting capacity in order to permit specialization. Because so many reporters were involved, it became particularly crucial for *Government Executive* editors to mandate that the same types of individuals be interviewed for each story. The list of sources included top management in each agency, field-level staff, GAO evaluators, representatives of labor unions, stakeholder groups, think tanks, congressional staff (appropriations and authorizing committees), and others.

Managers Survey

In year 3 of the federal project, a survey of managers was conducted for the first time in order to get a perspective on agency management from line staff. The focus in this questionnaire was on the perspectives of agency managers concerning the key management areas under review. For example, we were concerned with the extent to which strategic plans and visions identified at the top of the organization had percolated through the various management layers. The survey also focused on the extent to which these managers perceived that they had financial and performance information when they

needed it, possessed the tools to manage human resources, and had sufficient managerial flexibility. Each agency identified one hundred managers
that the survey would be sent to. These managers were geographically and
organizationally representative. The survey included seventy-seven questions covering all of the management areas under review. On average, the
response rate was approximately 60 percent for the seven agencies evaluated
during the 2000–2001 project year.

Although efforts were made on a less systematic basis to get manager-
level information for states and local governments, nothing as comprehensive as this manager's survey was attempted because of resource limitations.
It was only possible to conduct such a survey of federal agencies because of
the relatively limited number of agencies that were reviewed annually.

Converting Data Collected into Results

Data collection was a crucial step. A remaining challenge—as significant as
any confronted during the project—concerned how to organize these data in
a way that would permit legitimate results. This was critical to arriving at
valid grades. There were two key characteristics crucial to the consistency
and therefore to the validity of the grading process. The first was thorough-
ness. Each of the entities (states, localities, or federal agencies) had to be
evaluated according to all of the criteria relevant to that type of entity. It was
simply not possible to do a fair job of grading these governments or agencies
unless all relevant criteria were reviewed. If in financial management, for
example, we decided to consider the accuracy of forecasting for one state but
not for another, clearly this could bias our results. This standard of thor-
oughness meant that it was crucial to relate all information from all sources
into appropriate criteria.

Second, and related, each of these agencies or governments needed to be
evaluated by reviewing the same kind of information. As noted above, multiple sources of data were used for each of the entities. Just as we could not
look at some criteria and not others, neither could we use some sources of
data and not others. This means that the lack of key documents, for example,
would be cause for concern. But perhaps most importantly, the reporting
process had to be consistent and systematic. The same types of government
officials needed to be interviewed for each city, for example. In the federal
process, as noted above, multiple reporters were involved in the interview
process; the consistency of sources, then, became a key means by which
fairness could be promoted.

Once data were collected and sorted by categories, it remained for project staff to establish preliminary grades for each of the categories. Any grading process is inherently subjective. Indeed, conclusions could have been drawn and lessons learned about management in these governments and agencies even if no grades had been awarded. Grades, however, get people's attention. For that reason, the Pew Charitable Trusts, as well as the university and magazine partners, became convinced that the grades were an essential part of the process. They would provide an easy "hook" for public consumption as well as incentives for the recipients (and potential future recipients) to do well.

Before discussing the grading process further, it is important to understand what the grades themselves represent. They are an attempt to sort these agencies and governments into categories with those that are most similar in terms of managerial performance. As *Government Executive* quite aptly noted, "An A doesn't mean perfection and a D doesn't mean virtual failure. The grades are better viewed as an indication of the company it keeps, that is, whether its management capabilities place it in the top, middle or lower tier" (2001: 11) when these governments or agencies are compared to the management criteria that we are using.*

Moreover, a lower grade does not always mean that the agency or government has the ability to do any better. If the grades themselves are a statement of managerial results (asking the question "What is happening?"), it is also incumbent on the graders to explain *why* it is happening (asking the question "What would need to happen to improve management?"). For example, a given government may not make information available to managers where and when needed because of a lack of investment in IT resources

---

*Project staff made a specific choice to use letter grades to display the relative differences between entities for a number of reasons. Some other publications, including the earlier *Financial World* analyses of cities and states, had rank-ordered these governments (for example, states from 1 to 50). We decided that the nature of the analysis was such that we could not draw any narrow distinctions between the governments or agencies but that we could reasonably sort them into categories. While there was little way to present any meaningful difference between the 25th- and 26th-ranked state, for example, we did think it possible to establish some significant difference between states in the top category, those in the next level down, and so forth—thus, the very apt discussion of sorting entities in terms of the "company they keep." Even after the decision was made to organize the entities into categories (as opposed to rank ordering) we still needed to resolve how to label these different categories. The decision to use grades (as opposed, say, to "stars" or to some kind of descriptive categories—"top-rated" or "managerially challenged") was primarily influenced by the relative accessibility of grades to the public.

or because, even though sufficient funds have been expended for computer systems, it does a poor job of directing these resources to the appropriate place in the organization. The ultimate result (which is that key managers do not have the information) is the same in either case, and the grade would be the same in either case. But the solution in one case may be to make more resources available; in the other, it would be to make better use of the resources that have already been made available.

The Analytical Process Itself

How were the data themselves analyzed? In every case, development of the grades was a collaborative process involving both the academic and journalistic partners, including two steps. The first step was developing preliminary grades. The second was validating these grades through a subsequent grade validation process. The process for the state and local grading and the federal agency grading were a bit different, so they should be discussed separately.

State and Local Process

For each of the management categories, grades were arrived at separately by the journalists at *Governing* and academics at the Maxwell School. The Maxwell School grades were based primarily on the management questionnaire, on documentary analysis, and on validation follow-ups. Empirical assessments, based on careful coding and ranging from descriptive statistics to more complex techniques such as regression and fuzzy logic, were the foundation of the Maxwell grades. *Governing* grades were informed by the survey and other data collected but also by the many interviews conducted by reporters. Final grades were the product of consensus between academic and journalistic assessments.

This consensus, however, masks a great deal of energy expended by all of the actors in striving to ensure valid results. The use of "fuzzy logic" (an unfortunate name for a sophisticated technique) is one example, particularly for the analysis of financial management and human resource management systems.* Fuzzy logic, or fuzzy set theory, is a multivalued logic that applies a human-like way of thinking to evaluate complex problems through analysis of ambiguous or imprecise information by application of decision

---

*This explanation was provided by Sally Selden and William Kittredge. The refined fuzzy logic methodology they apply is explained in Ammar and Wright (2000).

rules. Fuzzy set theory is a generalization of classical ("crisp") set theory whereby a fuzzy set is defined by a function in [0,1] over a set of elements. In the classical representation, the value would be forced to be one or the other. In fuzzy logic, on the other hand, the function maps such that an evaluation measure can have degrees of membership in two adjacent categories. That is, measures that cannot be defined precisely—that depend on their context— are placed on a continuum representing the degree to which any given observation belongs in a "category," allowing for gradual transition among adjacent sets. Fuzzy set theory thus differs from classical theory in terms of both membership and boundaries since in fuzzy set theory an element may belong partially to a set and the boundaries in fuzzy set theory are blurred. Finally, a fuzzy logic conclusion is not stated as either true or false, but rather as being true to a certain degree.

Fuzzy set theory offers several advantages to the analysis of management systems. First, it provides an alternative way of representing impreciseness. It allows us to view concepts of possibility and vagueness separate from probabilistic or random uncertainty. Second, the technique permits the combination of numerical data with subjective opinion. Third, the set approach allows the nonlinear integration of measurements and interactions between measurements by applying a consistent set of rules. Application of such multivalent rule-based models in the natural sciences and engineering applications have demonstrated stability and robustness in the production of repeatable results from inexact data. Finally, fuzzy logic accommodates different sources of imprecision, including the context-sensitivity of expert opinion and the indistinctness of rule-of-thumb choices, as well as imperfections in data. Therefore, the data obtained through surveys of government managers about management activities and behavior can be incorporated into ratings of government management along our established set of evaluation criteria. The large numbers of governments surveyed by the GPP provided rich ground for the application of such analytical techniques.

The journalists from *Governing* used a separate process to assign draft grades. The journalistic grades were based on data that emphasized the survey less and other sources more heavily. Since the survey represented the state or locality's own story and these other sources included many documents and interviews external to the government, bringing the two together sometimes highlighted conflicts between the academics and journalists in terms of particular grades. Indeed, the process of grading was largely one through which consensus was reached where possible but where these differences caused each side to look more carefully at the grade in question. By and large, it is fair to say that the highest and lowest grades were assigned in cases where all sources and all graders were uniformly pointing in the same direction; areas of disagreement tended to cluster in the center of the grade distribution. There were no cases in which one set of graders argued for an "A," for example, while the other believed a "C" to be most accurate.

Federal Process

On the federal side, a slightly different process was used in years 1 and 2 than for year 3. For the first two years, independent evaluations were done by *Government Executive* reporters and relevant staff at the Maxwell School. The academic researchers reached their conclusions based primarily on the analysis of the management survey and external documents. The reporters based their grades primarily on information derived from interviews. In every case, agencies were rated against each of the criteria in each category. The focus of the process was on resolving differences between reporters and academic researchers. A crucial point to keep in mind is that no conclusions were reached about these agencies independent of the management criteria. Differences were resolved in meetings attended by representatives of both the magazine and the Maxwell School. A senior research associate from the Maxwell School and the project editor from *Government Executive* attended every meeting in order to minimize the possibility that criteria would be applied inconsistently across agencies.

In year 3, professors and graduate students at The George Washington University drafted preliminary grades, informed by substantial interaction with relevant *Government Executive* reporters in addition to access to the management survey, the managers survey, and other documents. A detailed process of data sorting was imposed on the university partners, who attached data from all sources (including the management survey, the managers' survey, documents, and interview results) to appropriate criteria. Preliminary grades were developed as a result of a systematic analysis of these data; again, the goal was to sort the agencies into appropriate categories based on their management capacity.

George Washington University staff ultimately presented the results of this analysis in summary "grading justifications" on each agency, which were subjected to two levels of review. First, *Government Executive* staff (including, most significantly, the reporter assigned to prepare the story on that agency) reviewed the summary. *Government Executive* staff noted any inaccuracies in the descriptions, and these were corrected. In the (rare) case that such an inaccuracy justified a change in the preliminary grade, that occurred. Subsequent to this internal validation, conclusions and grades were reviewed by an advisory panel made up of federal management experts, including many former high-ranking government officials. These were asked to look for cases where they believed that a mismatch existed between descriptions and grades, or places where they thought criteria might have been applied inconsistently. In cases where this board identified potential issues, the grades and descriptions were reviewed again before final grades were developed.

The entire grading process, at both the state and local and federal levels, was fraught with difficulty. A Herculean effort was expended in trying to ensure that the grading process was simultaneously consistently applied and fair. In the end, some grades may have been wrong. Indeed, all project staff were much more comfortable with our ability to "tell the stories" of each government or agency than we were to translate this story into letter grades. In the end, however, we are convinced that even the grades that may have been wrong were not far removed from reality. In other words, no one got a "B" that deserved a "D," or vice-versa. Our confidence in the results stems from two factors. First, the sheer quantity and breadth of the data (not to mention the number of separate criteria in each category) ensured a comprehensive base for the analysis and the grade that was unparalleled. Second, because academics, journalists, and outside experts (in the case of the federal grades) were involved, there were many checks along the way that minimized the likelihood that significant errors would result.

Finally, it is worth noting that only in a miniscule number of cases did any of the governments or agencies challenge the grades that appeared in the magazines, thus giving the grades face validity. In fact, if substantial challenges had occurred, it would have certainly caused us to fundamentally change the grading process. We did not, however, find it necessary to do this.

Conclusion

In the final analysis, the conclusions reached as a result of the GPP and FPP are only as good as the data collected and the care with which we analyzed results. When dealing with something as messy as government management, and with essentially a moving target, it is simply not possible to capture pure objective reality. In this chapter we have tried to convey two main ideas: first, that we went to great pains to use multiple methods of data collection in an effort to ensure that our conclusions as to "what's going on" in these agencies were not dependent on a single source but were validated using multiple

sources; and second, that we tried to avoid the probability of reaching er-
roneous conclusions through slavish attention to the criteria and the use of
multiple analysts and multiple methods of analyzing data.

The grades, of course, are only part of the story. The stories that appeared in the magazines as well as the academic analysis focused on key
lessons that could be learned about federal and state/local management as a
result of data collected by project staff. In the next two chapters we will
present not only the grades but also the detailed findings by management
areas for both state and local governments (Chapter 5) and federal agencies
(Chapter 6) studied since the onset of the project. After this, we will move on
to a discussion of the broader management lessons that came out of the
project.

5 | State and Local Findings

When the grades for government management were released each year of the Government Performance Project (GPP), press and editorial coverage demonstrated that management capacity and effectiveness are issues that can attract and hold public attention. Response from the governments included in the analyses demonstrated that the management systems of government are viewed as important platforms for improved performance. Significantly, the response also demonstrated that elected officials and other public managers believe that management systems are one of the elements of public performance that can be changed and redesigned in the pursuit of higher performance levels; they are a public policy tool. These attitudes are reflected in what states told us about performance data: forty-four reported that governors have a high demand for this kind of information; thirty-one reported that state legislators share this demand; and nineteen say that their citizens want it. Thirty-one states told us that performance information is frequently used in making budget allocation decisions. In short, understanding performance is on everyone's mind.

This chapter and the two that follow are about the numerous and complex lessons behind the GPP performance assessments. They include lessons about the systems the project analyzed, about commitment to performance in the governments studied, about comparisons among governments and across levels of government, about leadership, and about the political and public environments in which public management occurs. Some lessons are broadly overarching: they concern integration among the systems and the relationships between leadership and management capacity. We take up these broad crosscutting issues again in Chapter 7. There are also lessons that are more specific to federal agencies, state governments, or local governments. In this chapter, we examine the major lessons learned about the systems that were the focus of the analysis in state and local governments (GPP). In Chapter 6 we will review the detailed results for the three years of the federal project (FPP).

As we explained in Chapter 1, the GPP involved a collaboration between Syracuse University, which had responsibility for the academic dimensions of the project, and *Governing* magazine, which conducted journalistic reporting. During the course of the project, all fifty states were reviewed and graded twice by the academic and journalistic partners in the first and the third years of the project (see Table 5.1). In year 2, the project focused on thirty-five cities (see Table 5.2). In Table 5.3, we summarize these results by identifying the high, low, and average grades for states and cities by management area. The body of this chapter will present the key findings of these endeavors by management system—human resources, financial, information technology, and physical asset management. The chapter will conclude with a brief discussion of the overall state and local management environment and will discuss the importance of viewing our findings as part of a unified view of government management.

Financial Management Capacity (FM)

The criteria for assessing financial management, as do the criteria analyzing the other management systems, look carefully for longer-term strategic capabilities in government. The ability to plan for resource allocation, to set careful objectives and timelines, and to accurately forecast the resources that will be available to government are all linked, in this analysis, to the ability to build a capacity for performance. In light of this, the key findings of the GPP include:

1. *Financial management received higher grades than any other system in both state and local governments.* As noted above, financial management systems lend themselves to analysis more readily than do some of the other systems analyzed. The simple reality of dealing with numbers and budgets gives financial management a level of clarity and description that is more difficult to attain in information technology management. For example, the Governmental Accounting Standards Board's GAAP (generally accepted accounting principles) make state finances more transparent and comparable. Most states use them, and state accounting and financial reporting practices continue to improve. Budgets are also one of the most widely discussed aspects of governmental activity; they are broadly disseminated and are frequent parts of public policy debate. (Sixty-six percent of states report that they use at least three techniques for sharing budget projections with the public.)

It should also be noted that the years of the GPP analysis included relatively good economic times. Since governments were not under unusual fiscal stress, they were not as tempted to resort to questionable financial management practices as they might have been had the economy been worse. As explained in Chapter 3, our criteria-based system cannot control

Table 5.1. State Grades, 1999 and 2001

States	Average		FM		HR		IT		CM		MFR	
AL	D	C−	D+	C+	C−	D+	F	D+	D−	D+	D	C−
AK	C	C	C	C	C−	C	C−	C−	C+	C	C−	B
AZ	C	C+	B−	C	C+	C	B−	C+	D+	C+	D+	B−
AR	C−	C	B−	B−	C+	C	D	C−	C	C	D	C−
CA	C−	C+	C−	B−	C−	C	C−	C−	C−	C+	C+	B−
CO	C+	C+	C	C+	B	B−	C	C+	C	B	C	C
CT	C−	C	C−	C	C−	C	D+	C−	C+	B−	D+	C+
DE	B	B+	A−	A−	B	B	B	B	B	B+	B	B
FL	C+	B−	B	B	C+	B−	B	B+	C	B−	C−	C+
GA	C+	B−	C+	B−	B−	B−	C+	B−	C	B−	C	C+
HI	C−	C	C−	C	C−	C	C−	C	B−	B	F	C−
ID	C	B−	B−	C+	C	B	C−	C−	B−	B−	D+	B
IL	B−	B	B+	B+	B	B	C	B−	B−	B	D+	C+
IN	C+	B−	B	B−	C+	B	C	B−	C	B−	C	B−
IO	B	B+	A−	A−	B+	B+	B+	A−	B−	B+	C+	B
KS	B−	B	B−	B−	B+	B+	C	C+	B	B	C+	A−
KY	B	B+	B+	A−	B	B+	B	B+	A−	B+	C+	B+
LA	B−	B−	B−	C	C+	B	B	B+	B	B	C−	B−
ME	C	B−	B−	B−	C+	B−	C	C+	C−	B−	C	B−
MD	B	B+	A−	A−	B	B	B−	B	A−	A	C	B
MA	B−	C+	B	B−	C+	B−	C	C	B+	C+	C	C
MI	B+	A−	A−	A−	B+	B+	B	B+	B+	A−	B+	A−
MN	B	B	A−	A−	C+	C+	B	B	A−	B+	B	B
MS	C+	C+	B	B	C+	B−	C	D+	B	C	C−	C+
MO	A−	B+	A−	B+	B	B+	A−	A−	A	B+	B+	A−
MT	B−	C+	B	B	B−	C+	C	C	B+	C+	B−	C
NB	B	B−	B+	A−	B−	C	B−	B−	A−	B	C+	C+
NV	C+	C	B	B−	D	D+	C	C	B+	B	C	C−

Table 5.1. *Continued*

States	Average		FM		HR		IT		CM		MFR	
NH	C+	C	B−	C+	B	C+	D+	D	C	C+	C	C
NJ	B−	B−	B−	B−	C−	C−	B−	B−	B+	A−	B−	B
NM	C−	C+	C−	C+	B−	B−	D+	C	D	C−	C	C+
NY	C−	C+	D+	C+	C	C+	D+	C−	C−	C+	C	B
NC	B	B	B	B	B+	B+	B−	B	B+	B	C	B+
ND	B−	B−	B	B−	B−	B	D	C−	B+	B	B−	B−
OH	B	B	B+	B+	B	B	C+	B	B	B	B	B−
OK	C	C	B−	C+	C−	C−	D+	D+	C	C	C−	B−
OR	B−	C+	B	B−	C+	C	B+	B	B−	B−	C+	C
PA	B	B+	A−	A−	B	B+	B−	B	B	B	B	B+
RI	C−	C	B−	B−	F	C−	C	C	C+	C+	D	D
SC	B	B+	B+	A−	A−	A	B−	B	B−	C+	B	B
SD	B−	C+	B+	B−	C+	B−	D	D	B	B−	B	B
TN	B−	B−	B	C	C+	B−	C	B−	B−	C	B+	B+
TX	B	B	B	B+	B	B	B+	A−	C	B	B	B−
UT	A−	A−	A	A	B+	B−	B+	B+	A	A−	B+	A
VT	B−	B−	B	B	B−	C	B−	B	B	B−	C	C+
VA	A−	B+	A	B+	B	B+	A−	A−	A	B+	A−	A−
WA	A−	A−	A−	B+	B+	A−	B+	A−	A	A−	A	A
WV	C+	C	B	B−	C+	C+	C	C	C+	C	C	C−
WI	B	B−	C+	C+	B+	A−	C	C	A−	B+	B	B−
WY	C	C	C+	B−	B−	C+	C	C+	C+	D	D+	C−

Headings are abbreviations of the five systems studied. Average is the unweighted average of five grades.

Table 5.2. City Grades, 2000

City	Average	FM	HR	IT	CM	MFR
Anchorage	C	C+	C	C	B−	C−
Atlanta	C+	B−	B−	D+	C	B−
Austin	A−	A	A−	B	A−	A−
Baltimore	B−	B+	C+	C	B	B
Boston	B−	B−	C−	B	B+	C+
Buffalo	C−	C	D	C	C−	D+
Chicago	B−	B	C−	B−	B+	C+
Cleveland	C	B−	C−	C−	B−	C
Columbus	C	B−	C−	D+	B−	D
Dallas	C+	B+	C	D+	B−	B
Denver	B−	B+	B−	C+	B−	B−
Detroit	B−	B−	B−	B−	C	B−
Honolulu	B	B−	C	B+	A−	B
Houston	C+	B+	C	C−	B−	B−
Indianapolis	B+	B	A−	B	B+	A−
Jacksonville	B−	B	C+	C	B	B
Kansas City	B−	B+	B	C	B+	B−
Long Beach	B	A−	C	B	B	B−
Los Angeles	C	B−	C−	C−	C+	C−
Memphis	C+	B	D	C	B	B−
Milwaukee	B	B+	C+	B−	B+	A−
Minneapolis	B+	A−	B	A−	B+	B−
Nashville	C+	B	B	D+	C+	C−
New Orleans	C−	C−	F	B−	B−	D+
New York City	B	B	B−	B	B+	B
Philadelphia	B	B−	B−	B+	B−	B
Phoenix	A	A	A	A−	A	A
Richmond	C+	B	C	C	C−	C+

Table 5.2. *Continued*

City	Average	FM	HR	IT	CM	MFR
San Antonio	B	B+	B+	B−	B	B+
San Diego	B	B+	C	C	B+	A−
San Francisco	C+	B	C	C+	C+	C
San Jose	B−	B+	C	C	A−	C+
Seattle	B	B+	B	B	B+	B
Virginia Beach	B+	A−	B	B	A−	B
Washington	C+	B−	B−	C+	C	C+

for the economic environment; thus, in our grading periods governments may have received relatively high grades in financial management because of the positive economic circumstances they enjoyed. Post-2002 results would undoubtedly be different.

States are the only level of government for which comparable findings are available for two years, and the results from 1999 and 2001 are similar in many ways. Table 5.1 presents these results. In both years, about one-fifth of the states achieved a grade of A or A− in financial management. There were no regional or partisan patterns in the high-capacity states. Some states demonstrated significant improvement in the two-year period: both New York and Alabama, for example, moved up at least a full grade—New York from a D+ to a B−, Alabama from a D+ to a C+. Both states were at the bottom of the grading spectrum in the first year of grading the states. Only nine of the states in analyzed in 1998 received a grade of C or lower in financial management, and eleven of the states in 2001 received similar grades. At the city level, only three of the thirty-five largest cities examined received a C or lower (Table 5.2). This can be attributed in part to the visibility and measurability inherent in the area of financial management (what can be measured gets done better), but it probably also reflects the likelihood that governments have learned from past experiences.

At both the state and local levels, there is good evidence of improved budgetary decision-making information and processes, better forecasting capabilities, and better contingency planning. In some cases, it must be noted, the improvements built on a sad earlier base: several large cities— New York, Washington, and Detroit, for example—were forced to rebuild failed financial management capability. States such as New York continue to

Table 5.3. State and Local Grades, 1999 and 2001

	States		Cities
	1999	2001	
Financial Management			
Average grade	B	B	B
High grade	A	A	A
Low grade	D+	C	C−
Capital Management			
Average grade	B−	B−	B
High grade	A	A	A−
Low grade	D−	D	C−
Human Resources			
Average grade	B−	B−	C+
High grade	A−	A	A
Low grade	F	D+	D
Information Technology			
Average grade	C+	B−	C+
High grade	A	A	A−
Low grade	D	D	D+
Managing for Results			
Average grade	C+	C+	B−
High grade	A−	A−	A
Low grade	F	D	D

struggle with the politics of budgetary approval; they have not passed a budget on time for years. But overall, state budgets are usually timely (forty-four out of fifty adopted their last budget in advance of the fiscal year), and structural balance is much more the norm than in past years. Fourteen states still used nonrecurring fiscal resources to balance their FY2000 budgets, however.

2. *When key decision makers are involved, planning and performance go hand in hand.* States generally attempt to forecast revenues and expenditures, though the quality of these forecasts is uneven. Some states (Maryland, for example) conduct strategic planning and forecasting for budget and revenue with joint executive-legislative teams, permitting the growth of a solid foundation for budgetary understanding and debate. Some states have found that good information about the future fiscal implications of programs supports sound legislative decision making, and almost all states

make such assessments. At the same time, legislation or procedures mandating some connection between the budget and performance information is in place in a large majority of the states. The growth in attention to describing anticipated impact of expenditures, tracking and measuring impact, and using that information in future decision-making processes generally describes governments that have developed information management capacity in tandem with financial management strength.

In addition, states have found that cost accounting tools can provide valuable information that allows governments to prioritize their spending—all but three states use cost accounting to some extent—but states find the tools difficult to implement and do not understand cost accounting well. Thus, progress here, while real, has been slow. Utah is one state where cost accounting has enabled cost-effective decisions to be made.

And finally, spending flexibility is consistent with financial accountability and can support performance. States in general are moving toward giving agencies more flexibility in managing money, sometimes even coincidental with attempting to hold them accountable for achieving results.

3. *Most states take advantage of good times to prepare for bad.* The top performing states in both years of the GPP analysis (Maryland, Utah, Washington, and Missouri), as well as states such as Virginia that have traditionally relied on financial management as the glue for their broader management base, not only maintain a good structural balance between revenue and expenditures but plan carefully for utilization of surpluses and for a contingency cushion. In our grading period, states were taking advantage of good economic times to put money away in rainy-day funds (funds set aside in good or surplus years to offset budget shortfalls in harder times).

Despite the common practice of contingency planning, there continues to be wide variation in standards and practices for contingency funds. There was substantial disparity in use and size of rainy-day funds across the states in both years, and this disparity was mirrored in the city findings. Although there is not complete consensus about the figure, many analysts have argued that a set-aside of 5 percent is appropriate for planning purposes (Joyce, 2001). Even after ten years of remarkable economic growth, however, in 2000 the average rainy-day set-aside had decreased slightly from the 1998 number —from 4.30 to 3.86 percent. Some states were dramatic outliers—Alaska on the negative end and Nebraska with a set-aside of about 36 percent are examples. Alaska is a somewhat unusual case since a substantial Constitutional Budget Reserve allows drawdowns to meet budget shortfalls. Drawdowns are not unlimited, however, and there has been a consistent pattern of budget shortfalls in Alaska. It presents an excellent example of the need for careful budgetary analysis and planning.

Cities also presented wide-ranging experiences in rainy-day fund use. In a group in which two-thirds of those analyzed received either an A or a B in financial management, the experience with rainy-day planning and set-asides ranged from none—due either to consistent overspending or to legal limitations—to nearly 30 percent in Indianapolis. Furthermore, the cities demonstrated significant disparity in ability to deal with the thorny issues of retirement and benefit funds and overtime costs for services such as police and fire protection. Cities such as Milwaukee, Los Angeles, and Philadelphia struggle with these problems and will undoubtedly continue to do so for the foreseeable future. Leading cities in financial management like Minneapolis and Phoenix are notable for rigorously professional financial planning and for relying on extensive contingency analysis in the decision process.

The cities that did not do well in financial management—only three cities received a C or C−—suffered from a variety of maladies. Political or legal limits constrain the ability of cities such as Buffalo and New Orleans to control salary costs and to bring in revenue from sources such as property taxes. In these cases, good management is sometimes secondary to coping.

Capital and Infrastructure Management Capacity (CM)

Overall, most of the governments examined by the GPP did not do badly in the tough business of capital and infrastructure management. As Table 5.3 shows, in both 1999 and 2001, the average state grade for capital management was a B−. The city average grade in 2000 was B. Effective capital management includes three core activities, each of which is critical. Planning for new or replacement structures and infrastructures is a lengthy and complex task involving large numbers of stakeholders, enormous budgets, and substantial intergovernmental coordination. Building to specification and within budget—whether it is a new city hall, government office space, roads, or bridges—while still meeting numerous regulatory demands, is equally complicated. Perhaps most difficult, however, is ensuring proper and timely maintenance of the structures once they are in place. Along these lines, our significant findings about physical asset management include:

1. *Vision and commitment are vital.* Capacity in capital and infrastructure management is closely linked to the issues discussed above in rainy-day fund management. Just as setting aside funds for a rainy day in good times is

difficult, so is investing for the future or repairing deteriorating capital structures if the problems do not appear to be immediate. Both activities require long-term vision and unwavering political will. Many observers argue that the similarities between rainy-day cushions and capital management funding extend further: if capital and infrastructure investments are to be properly monitored and maintained, they say, funding for the activities should come from a dedicated revenue source and not be taken from operating budgets. Despite the commonsense appeal of this approach, however, it remains an unusual practice for most governments.

Most states do engage in effective long-term planning for capital, but sometimes this planning gets derailed by the political attractiveness of capital "pork." Capital planning is a sound practice, but it is often not handled well politically; it is an obvious opportunity for pork-barrel spending. Capital planning can benefit from detailed, accurate information about the condition of the full inventory of existing facilities, but states often avoid collecting this data because in virtually every case it amounts to "bad news" for budgets.

2. *Maintenance too often gets short shrift.* In many cases, the relatively high average grades in capital management reflect solid planning and information-gathering efforts rather than actual project and maintenance funding. The biggest problem in the states is the underfunding of maintenance. Unfortunately, maintenance is not as sexy as new construction. It is also relatively easy to underfund maintenance, both because the amounts needed are so massive and because deferred maintenance rarely attracts attention. Governments typically do not do a good enough job of protecting funding for regular maintenance. Moreover, they don't always understand clearly what maintenance is required—up to 20 percent make condition assessments less often than every five years.

In major cities and in a large number of states, maintenance needs dramatically outstrip available funding, even in good economic times. One city estimated that 80 percent of facility maintenance and 66 percent of street maintenance costs were being deferred. Deferred maintenance—or no maintenance at all—was one of the most consistent problems in management found by the GPP. Indeed, in 2001 the state GPP survey revealed that fully one-fourth of the states were limited in their ability to plan for future maintenance expenses because they had either no capital improvement planning documents or documents that looked two years or less into the future.*

---

*For reference, the GPP 1999, 2000, and 2001 results are posted at the project website at www.maxwell.syr.edu/gpp.

The cities also display serious problems with deferred maintenance costs. Many of them do not know the total cost of deferred maintenance expenses or have consciously neglected infrastructure maintenance in favor of more visible new projects. Los Angeles provides one example. In 1999 it was able to repave only 220 miles of roadway from an inventory of 6,500 miles. Similarly, Kansas City—though exemplary in other ways—knows that actual annual maintenance costs are over $14 million but was able to budget only $4.5 million in 1999.

3. *Planning matters, but it must be closely linked to operations and mainte-nance.* As Table 5.1 demonstrates, the states examined by the GPP offer a variety of experiences and models in capital planning. For states, the experience ranges from the strong performances of Maryland (A) and Washington (A−) to the problematic situation in Alabama (D+). Overall, only three states lack formal plans altogether. The strong states are characterized by carefully managed and strategic long-term (ten-year) planning, by the ability to manage capital projects to budget, and by coordination between the executive and the legislature. Sound and reliable information gathering, which becomes a core part of the decision process, is also important. Alabama, on the other hand, lacks a planning process, struggles to coordinate very disparate agency capital planning activities, does not have adequate funding for either construction or maintenance, and—even with gubernatorial prodding—is several years from an effective attack on any of the above problems.

To a considerable extent, capital and maintenance shortfalls reflect a disconnect between executive branch planning processes and legislative decisions about the budget, or even a lack of coordination within the executive branch. Nearly 40 percent of the states reported in 2001, for example, that the legislature had either no role or a limited informal role in capital planning and priority setting. Seven states reported no planning coordination across their agencies. These disconnects are exacerbated by frequent failure to link or coordinate strategic planning to operating budgets—a problem reported by 64 percent of the states in 2001—and to coordinate capital planning with other strategic planning activities. Utah is one notable exception here, requiring that a proportion of facilities' replacement cost be preserved to meet maintenance needs. Indiana and Virginia have similar practices.

In the largest cities, capital planning and maintenance issues are very direct and immediate. Citizens observe potholes and deteriorating buildings daily; repairing them is a major and very symbolic government activity. As a result, cities take these management systems seriously, and many are creative in approaching planning and maintenance issues. Kansas City, for example, encourages citizens to make capital budget proposals online and publishes an easily accessible and understandable capital improvement plan. Milwaukee clusters capital projects around infrastructure networks and sites so that the area is viewed as a composite whole and each project is considered, not in isolation, but as a part of that whole.

Human Resources Management Capacity (HR)

Financial and capital management systems deal with the fiscal and physical assets of government; human resources management deals with the people. Increasingly, the fact that "human capital" is one of government's most significant resources is becoming more evident (Ingraham, Selden, and Moynihan, 2000; Walker, 2000). Moreover, as other government management systems benefited from good economic times and a consistent—or growing—revenue base, human resources management struggled with a shortage of people, talent, and expertise as governments fought to compete for scarce human resources.

For the fifty states, the average HR grade in 1999 was B— (see Table 5.3). This average, however, reflects one grade each of D and F, and twenty-two C's. Obviously, there were strong performers whose overall assessment offset these grades: there were one A— and seven B+'s among the 1999 grades. In 2001, HR grades improved slightly: there were one solid A (South Carolina) and two A—'s (Washington and Wisconsin). However, there were also twenty grades of C or lower. City grades also reflected difficulties with human resources management. In the 2000 survey of the thirty-five largest cities, over half received a grade of C or lower.

The cities in the 2000 survey also revealed wider variation in human resources management policies and processes than did the states. This is due largely to the presence of essentially unreformed patronage systems in some cities, as well as a variety of collective bargaining arrangements and structures. Grades ranged from a solid A (Phoenix) and two A—'s (Indianapolis and Austin) to two D's (Buffalo and Memphis) and one F (New Orleans). The cities with the lowest grades were generally those with either very rigid, older civil service systems or those that continued to be heavily influenced by patronage.

In the area of human resources management, our major findings are:

1. *The burden of rigid civil service systems persists.* A problem common to most levels of government was the continued reliance on a traditionally rigid

civil service system. Such systems, initially designed to exclude undue partisan and other external influences, are cumbersome and slow. Their excessive reliance on centralization and standardization decreases the ability of individual government agencies to respond to specialized mission needs and to demands for greater flexibility. In addition, the insular nature of civil service systems impedes their integration with other management systems and in some cases even causes managers and other public officials to consider them outside the realm of management. To be sure, there are examples of strongly decentralized systems in the states. Texas is one example, and Georgia, which abolished its central merit system in 1996, is another. Nonetheless, as a result of civil service issues, labor-management concerns, and other constraints, human resources management has consistently been one of the most problematic systems examined by the GPP.

State managers increasingly recognize that many civil service structures are not responsive to effective and flexible service delivery. Replacing rule-bound civil service systems with systems that allow flexibility and accountability is one major change in the way some state governments operate. There are substantial constraints to such reform efforts in many places, however. Not the least of these are union opposition and legislative barriers. Among the practices most likely to be reformed are testing (replacing a standardized application with more "applicant-friendly" approaches) and hiring (where the rule of 3 is starting to go by the boards). Increased flexibility in the hiring process and better use of technology have reduced the time it takes to fill open positions in state government. On the other hand, one of the areas of greatest future need is in the area of discipline and firing. The difficulty of dealing with poor performers continues in many states.

2. *The trend is toward a strategic balance between centralized and decentralized structures.* Human resources activities are most obvious on the front lines, but it is often difficult to understand the impact of the most important practices, such as hiring, firing, reward, and discipline at this level of the organization. Broad patterns of change are readily evident in both state and city government, however. For the states, the most notable change is the movement from one or the other end of the centralization-decentralization spectrum to a middle ground of strategic balance and sharing. In these settings, human resources management systems are shared responsibilities and authorities between the "center"—most often a central personnel agency —and individual agencies. The center retains authority for strategic direction and choice; the agencies receive the authority to implement and assess according to agency objectives and missions. Hiring is an obvious example: in

twenty-six states hiring is delegated to the agency level, but there are central guidelines for designing procedures. Such a system benefits from both the ability to emphasize core governmental values government-wide and the ability to define performance in less standardized and more agency-specific terms. Table 5.4 demonstrates this shift to the center in relation to a core component of performance: performance appraisal systems.

One exception to the shared balance trend is classification. Comparison of 1998 and 2000 data suggests that in the area of classification, states are moving toward more central involvement rather than less. In 1998, eight states had decentralized authority to agencies and managers for classification. In 2000, only two states decentralized authority for developing the classification system, and five indicated that authority was decentralized for job classifications and reclassifications.

3. *Once more, planning is vital.* Workforce planning represented one of the most serious difficulties encountered in human resources management at both the state and local levels. In particular, statewide personnel management often suffers from a lack of central information about the workforce and a failure to make decisions in a context of careful planning, but this may mask idiosyncratic efforts at the individual agency level that a government-wide analysis overlooks.

The need for sound workforce planning is particularly salient in an environment where state governments are increasingly finding themselves in competition for highly talented workers (Ingraham, Selden, and Moynihan, 2000). On average, states had almost 6,600 positions to fill in 1999: Virginia had 40,000 vacancies; Texas, 31,000; and North Carolina, 27,292. Some of these positions are newly created, but most are positions left vacant because employees leave voluntarily, retire, or are terminated. In 1999, voluntary turnover in state governments ranged from 2 to 20 percent. Facing competition for skilled labor, open positions, and growing turnovers, states implemented sometimes striking procedural changes to speed the hiring process. These included employment information and application on line, more flexible testing, and hiring and compensation incentives.

Despite the difficulties in recruiting in specialized areas and the hiring problems encountered in a generally tight labor market, few city governments had the capacity to consider long-term staffing and hiring needs.

There are, of course, exceptions. Austin, Texas, is notable for its workforce planning data and analysis; Washington State has a system that allows it to consider high-priority recruiting challenges and to shape strategies accordingly. Furthermore, workforce planning is an area that the states in

Table 5.4. Performance Appraisals: A Comparison of Authority in 1998 and 2000

Locus of authority	1998	2000
Centralized	25	18
Shared	6	34
Decentralized	17	9

N = Number of states: 1998 (49); 2000 (50).

particular have recognized as problematic and have moved to address. In the 2001 survey, the GPP found that one in four states had a formal workforce plan in place, up substantially from the 1998 survey. And finally, the cities, as did some of the states, have demonstrated the utility of technology in facilitating workforce planning, outreach and recruiting, and internal decision making and planning.

Information Technology (IT)

In the conceptual model outlined in Chapter 2, we argued that information technology and the issues associated with its strategic management would be closely related to the creation of management capacity and potential performance in the governments we studied. The analysis revealed that information technology is, indeed, central to effective management. Furthermore, the integrative ability that successful deployment and implementation of information technology provides is the underpinning for integration among other management systems.

Information technology management, however, is also hard to get right. When the first GPP surveys were completed, the specter of Y2K hung over the governments, and the initial grades indicated that there was good reason to be concerned. The average IT grade for the states in 1999 was C+; the grade was the same for the cities in 2000. In 2001, the average state grade was up to B− (Table 5.3). The problems identified in state and city governments were strikingly similar: antiquated systems, lack of coordination in design and purchase of technology systems, failure of systems to "speak" to one another, inadequate training for both technology personnel and end users, and inadequate funding to meet demand.

Some situations were dire (no information technology staff at all, for example, in one major city), while others provided strong lessons in careful planning and needs assessment. Minneapolis, for example, has made great strides in capitalizing on the integrative power of a good information technology system. At the same time, governments more generally were focusing strongly on bringing information technology systems and their management up to higher standards. As Table 5.1 demonstrates, in the 2001 survey, state IT grades increased from the 1999 level in thirty states. This was the greatest increase of any of the management systems studied.

Overall, we have found that the qualities that contribute to high capacity in information technology management include efforts to coordinate and focus information technology planning and management activities, sustained and frequently revisited analysis of needs and likely future demands, adequate funding for new systems and architecture, and useful training for both technical personnel and end users. Governments that lack these characteristics have less capacity, not only in information technology but also in other areas of management that information technology supports. Common trends in information technology management are:

1. *Increased reliance on strategic planning for information technology.* As in other management systems, planning matters—but information technology planning is particularly challenging because time is limited. Technology changes very fast, and systems are often doomed to be outdated by the time governments launch them. In 2001, forty states said they could generate a request for proposal (RFP) in less than six months, and roughly half reported that they could move from the RFP to system roll-out in less than six months. Strategic information technology plans vary widely in quality, perhaps as a result of the speed at which the information technology field is developing and because it can be very difficult to predict needs. Despite these challenges, 82 percent of the states—a significant increase from 1999—indicated that they had strategic information technology plans currently in place in 2001. More than 60 percent review these plans annually or semiannually. Information technology is also a component of statewide strategic plans in twenty-nine states.

2. *Increased centralization and coordination of information technology management and training.* While information technology traditionally has been decentralized, it is consistently and rapidly being centralized and coordinated across states—a notably different trend from the shifts in the locus of authority for human resources management. Many governments are adopting standardization rules and policies. The addition of a chief information officer position and staff was a frequent move among the states, creation of the position often being a key signal of the trend toward greater centralization of technology decision making. In 2001, when the average state IT grade increased to a B−, forty-two states reported that a chief information officer

was in place, and thirty-five reported that they considered their information technology management to be "highly centralized."

The other side of this coordination effort is that participation in the design and development of new information technology systems is relatively limited in many states. The 2001 survey revealed that the legislature (or its representatives) and the governor's office were rarely involved in these processes. End users assisted in planning in about half the states, and individual agencies were involved in almost all cases. It is also notable that there is a substantial participation gap between design (50%) and implementation (77%) for the chief information officer; that is, the CIO's participation was much more extensive in the implementation stage of information technology projects than in the earlier design phases.

3. *Integration is a key concern.* Our 1999 analysis revealed that many states were replacing at least one central information technology system. Some states were engaged in major systems improvements. Many of these governments relied on specific solutions to limited problems—new human resources management software, for example—to address existing problems in each management system. Such focused systems were costly and time-consuming to implement and train for; they also did not provide the platform for integration with other information management systems present or planned for in the government. As a result, many of the barriers to coordination and integrated decision making that the management systems themselves had posed earlier are now reinforced once again by new software and technology. Well under half of the states (40%) have made serious efforts to create a coherent architecture for integrating their management systems, including performance information and managing for results. This situation may be improving, however, as thirty-nine states report that formal standards governing kinds of technology that may be purchased are now being enforced.

4. *Continued struggle over how to gauge the benefits of information technology systems relative to their costs.* States in general are still very much behind the curve when it comes to doing detailed prior assessments of the benefits that a given information technology system will provide, and they may be even further behind in trying to hold vendors to performance standards after the fact. Some states, such as Pennsylvania, Ohio, and Maine, stand out as leaders in this area.

5. *Increasing use of the Internet—not only to provide information but also for transactions with citizens.* Washington, which received an IT grade of A in 2001, has made notable progress in the area of integration and has also

extended the integration to the way citizens are able to interact with the state Internet site. A new system will permit seamless movement from agency to agency and application to application, the use of a single password, and greater speed and simplicity in online transactions. At least eight other states have also made significant strides in this area.

Managing for Results (MFR)

Linking managing for results to performance has most often focused on the results part of the title—the performance measurement issues endemic to public organizations. Indeed, much of the literature proceeded from the apparent assumption that if the measures were right, all else would fall into place. The GPP analysis emphasizes again the intervening role of capacity. Ingraham and Moynihan note that "performance measurement, by itself, is an activity that produces information. . . . The distinction between measurement and management highlights that measurement systems provide information about performance, but do not guarantee good performance" (Moynihan and Ingraham, 2001a). Effective management for results creates capacity for improved performance; that is, the progress to which performance measures may be applied.

In addition, effective managing for results systems ensure, first, that performance information is of a good quality, and second—and very significantly—that it will be used in decision-making processes. Because effective managing for results both assists in the generation of quality information and also ultimately depends upon it, as a system it can serve as an integrating influence among the other management systems of government. Managing for results serves as a vehicle for effective leadership because the strategic-planning and goal-setting activities on which it depends require a coherent and long-term vision for the future as well as substantive steps for achieving that vision.

Despite the significance of effective managing for results to performance improvement and system integration, it is one of the management systems that all levels of government find problematic. The cities in the GPP analysis received an average MFR grade of B−. State governments averaged C+ and readily acknowledged the difficulties they confronted in creating effective systems. The grade range for managing for results was quite dramatic. For states, the high grade for both years of the analysis was an A−, but one state received an F, and there were several Ds as well.

Even though the average grades are similar, there were differences in the two state surveys. Strategic planning for at least some state agencies occurs in most of the states. In 1997, however, only seventeen states reported preparing statewide strategic plans; by 1999, that number had increased to twenty-nine. Processes for arriving at the strategic plan vary substantially. Some state plans are produced in conjunction with the budget; some are a combination of individual agency plans; in still others, the governor's office is the leading actor. As this suggests, there is variation in the degree of central coordination and direction—and, indeed, in the extent to which the overall plan represents a unified state vision. The participation of the legislature or of legislative staff in any of these activities is the exception rather than the rule.

While there is a strong reliance on output measurement rather than on broader outcome measures, several states—such as Utah, Virginia, North Carolina, and Oregon—have carefully designed systems that consider both and that attempt to link outcomes to broader and crosscutting policy objectives. Minnesota's "BIG" plan identifies the agencies responsible for achieving each of the broad targets, and each agency plan incorporates goals from the BIG plan into its own. Michigan uses outcome measures in its performance budgeting activities and documents. Iowa, a strong performer in managing for results, relies heavily on setting challenging goals and constructing careful measures that allow the governor, the legislature, and citizens to understand progress toward their achievement.

In addition to the difficulties posed by moving from output measures to outcomes, states report serious difficulties in using the information generated by performance management systems outside of the executive branch. Performance reports are publicly available in 80 percent of the states that engage in managing for results. Most states responding to the survey reported, however, that the highest demand for performance information came from the governor's office and executive agency heads. In earlier work (1993), Joyce reported similar findings and concluded that the most effective use of performance information may well be at the staff level. At the same time, many states note that additional legislative involvement would be preferable. Certainly, if one characteristic of effective leadership is a fully functional performance management system, bridging the boundaries between legislative and executive is an important objective for leaders in both of these branches.

Cities not only attained a better overall average grade than other levels of government (see Table 5.3) but also displayed a wider range of strategies. To some extent, cities have the advantage in managing for results: the services they deliver are readily visible and understandable to citizens. Garbage pick-up and pothole repair are obvious examples. Cities have also made very good progress in understanding the relative utility of different levels and means of measurement and in crafting measures for specific audiences and targets. Seattle noted in its survey, for example, that "output measures are most useful to front-line management to assess productivity and efficiency. Outcome measures are also important on the front-line, but are more important for management, leadership, and policy makers." Indianapolis observed, "The objective is to further develop the meaningfulness of the performance measures, but just as importantly, to develop the management expertise in understanding, utilizing, and analyzing the information that the report provides."

Cities that excel in managing for results provide a broad set of examples on design and utilization of an effective system. Phoenix, one of five cities to receive an A or A−, is an exemplar of driving managing for results and performance values throughout the city, to all employees, and to many citizens who receive city services and participate in their evaluation. Phoenix is also one of the approximately 24 percent of the cities surveyed that clearly and consistently communicates results of actual performance against objectives and targets. Newspapers, newsletters, and brief readable reports are used to convey performance information to citizens in formats they can understand and use. Similar strategies are found in San Diego, Austin, and Indianapolis.

Because city services are so visible and so immediate to citizens, the experiences of cities that did not do well with managing for results systems are also very relevant to performance and performance assessment. Three of the thirty-five cities studied in 1999 received a D or a D+. In at least one case, the city simply saw no benefits from managing for results in good economic times. In others, resource constraints or lack of leadership undermined the effort. In still other cities that did not do well, there was a conscious backing away from the difficulties associated with measuring results. This was most true of efforts to use outcome measures rather than outputs. One city was blunt in this regard: "We generally find that when a Department or Division establishes an outcome base measure, it often discovers during the year that it does not have the ability to control or at least significantly influence the external variables that can and so often do play a major role in determining whether an outcome measure can be achieved or not."

Overall, cities relied on output measures three times as often as they attempted to construct and use more complex outcome measurement. Customer satisfaction indices are also frequently used (Moynihan, 2000). Without any question, the resource-intensive and complex nature of appropriate measurement is a significant deterrent to greater city reliance on managing for results as a decision-making tool. Nonetheless, all but a handful of the cities included in the GPP analysis recognized the benefits that effective managing for results could bring and were making serious efforts to improve their systems.

Some General Observations

In general, most state and local governments do understand the need for strong management capabilities, and many are giving effective management top priority in change and reform efforts. No single pattern for how and when leaders and managers have chosen to proceed toward better management objectives exists, however.. There is also no recipe for incorporating information about performance into managerial decision making; states use a wide array of approaches with varying degrees of success. For example, there are many legislative requirements for strategic planning at the statewide level, but there is substantial variation from state to state in terms of how seriously this is taken. The GPP found both strengths and weaknesses in all regions of the country, in both rich and poor states and cities, and across partisan lines.

In addition, it appears that some systems are either easier to manage or easier to "get right" than others. According to the GPP criteria, for example, financial management systems are consistently one of the best-performing systems at all levels of government. In 1999, ten states received A's in financial management; that number was eight in 2001. Five cities received the grade in 2000. Several explanations may account for this: financial management systems are clearly specified, and budgetary issues are communicated with some clarity; financial management's concrete numbers are recognizable and understandable to citizens and elected officials; and budgetary processes frequently operate according to national standards that, if not universally accepted, are generally recognized. In contrast, managing for results systems, with less clear boundaries and less specific data, are almost universally problematic.

A corollary, however, is that most of the governments analyzed by the GPP showed variation across the management systems we studied. In 1999, only seventeen states had generally consistent grades across the systems; in 2000, a slightly larger proportion of the thirty-five largest cities demonstrated that consistency. Consistency is not necessarily a contributor to capacity but only marks position on the capacity range. In the case of the cities, several were consistently at the middle range. The more limited set of governments who were high capacity reached that level by doing well across all of the systems. Those few who had little capacity and potential for performance did poorly with all or most of the systems studied.

A lesson specific to city government is that elected officials—especially mayors—are linked to management and overall performance in a way that does not occur so obviously in state governments and federal agencies. The management initiatives of the mayor—often in conjunction with the city manager and the city council or commission—are understood to be linked very directly to service delivery and quality. Examples are provided by the mayors of Washington, New York, and Detroit and by the mayoral-manager team in Phoenix. This link is much more difficult to establish at the state and certainly at the federal level, where management champions are more difficult to connect directly to service and other performance factors.

The role of leadership as a factor in success cannot be overlooked, however. As our work proceeded and available information permitted the analysis of high-capacity state and local governments versus those with limited capacity, the significance of leadership emerged. As noted in an earlier chapter, the GPP did not study or measure leadership directly. Rather, we examined the creation of integrating mechanisms and systems within the governments and the creation of capacity for performance. Although the findings are preliminary and are based on an early stage of analysis, they are compelling.

The kinds of leaders and leadership teams we found in the GPP work did not resemble the leaders most commonly described in the vast literature related to private-sector leaders' styles, attributes, and strategies, or even those described in the more limited public-sector studies. Rather, these leaders were "grounded" leaders and teams, who pooled their talents and expertise to create and use opportunities for longer-term change and improvements in government.* They were critical to efforts at integration and capacity building, using their combined talents to provide vision, core values, and coordination to capacity building activities. They were "grounded" in the sense that they worked to overcome limited tenure and different organizational capacities by institutionalizing system connectors and by paying care-

---

*As some examples of leaders' styles, attributes, and strategies from a very large literature, see Bass (1985); Doig and Hargrove (1990); and Borins (2000). For a fuller discussion of leadership literature and discussion of early findings from the GPP, see Ingraham, Sowa, and Moynihan (2002).

ful attention to implementation. Both elected/appointed officials and career employees were crucial to these leadership efforts. Their joint commitment to effective government was a key factor toward reaching that goal.

Conclusion

In the earlier chapters of this book, we advanced the notion that management capacity in government organizations could be analyzed by examining the separate systems that broadly underpin management per se. We argued further that it would be possible to determine variations in those systems not only across similar units of government but within each unit of government as well. The first three years of the GPP did, in fact, reveal variation in capacity for performance. Grades ranged from A to F. All levels of government generally did better in financial management than in either human resources management or managing for results, and grades improved markedly for information technology management from one grading period to the next. They did not show such dramatic variation for the other systems.

We likewise see considerable variation in the management capacities of federal agencies. We will describe this in the following chapter.

6 | Federal Results

During the first three years of the GPP and FPP, twenty-seven federal agencies were reviewed and graded by the academic and journalistic partners. As noted in Chapter 1, *Government Executive* magazine has carried the journalistic side of the project since its inception. The academic end has been the responsibility first of Syracuse University and then of The George Washington University. This chapter will present the results of our analysis of federal agency results after the first three years of the project.

A couple of reminders are in order before we continue. First, as we noted in Chapter 4, our definition of *federal agency* includes the operating units of the federal government as opposed to, for example, cabinet departments. Accordingly, our focus has been on the Internal Revenue Service rather than the Treasury Department, or on the Food and Drug Administration rather than the Department of Health and Human Services. Cabinet departments are often "holding companies" for largely unrelated functions; it seemed to us to be much more relevant to consider agencies at the subcabinet level.

Given this definition, the agencies that we have looked at over the first three years, by year, are as follows (cabinet departments in parentheses, as applicable):

- 1998/1999 (publication in February 1999)—Food and Nutrition Service (Agriculture), Food Safety and Inspection Service (Agriculture), Customs Service (Treasury), Internal Revenue Service (Treasury), Health Care Financing Administration (Health and Human Services), Food and Drug Administration (Health and Human Services), Federal Aviation Administration (Transportation), Occupational Safety and Health Administration (Labor), Federal Housing Administration (Housing and Urban Development), Veterans Health Administration (Veterans' Affairs), Immigration and Naturalization Service (Justice), Patent and Trademark Office (Commerce), Environmental Protection Agency, Social Security Administration, Federal Emergency Management Agency.
- 1999/2000 (publication in March 2000)—United States Coast Guard (Transportation), Army Corps of Engineers (Army), National Park

Service (Interior), Office of Student Financial Assistance (Education), Veterans' Benefits Administration (Veterans' Affairs).

- 2000/2001 (publication in April 2001)—National Weather Service (Commerce), Bureau of Consular Affairs (State), United States Forest Service (Agriculture), Bureau of Indian Affairs (Interior), Administration for Children and Families (Health and Human Services), National Aeronautics and Space Administration, United States Postal Service.

In this chapter we will review the detailed results for the first three years of the federal project. Because the focus of the project on the federal side has evolved into giving great emphasis to results-based management, the managing for results findings will receive greatest emphasis. Each of the other issue areas—human resources management, financial management, information management, and physical asset management—will then be discussed. The chapter will conclude with a brief discussion of the overall federal management environment and discuss the importance of viewing these findings as part of a unified view of federal management as a unified whole. (A complete listing of the grades in all categories for the twenty-seven agencies can be found in Table 6.1).

Managing for Results (MFR)

As noted in Chapter 2, the criteria for managing for results have focused, through the history of the project, on several different activities:

- Strategic planning and mission definition;
- Performance measurement, focusing particularly on efforts to measure outcomes;
- Use of performance information to make decisions, to manage day to day affairs of the agency, and to report on accomplishments to stakeholders.

Over the three years, the average grade of agencies of agencies in managing for results has been a B−. This, however, masks a substantial amount of variation, as is indicated in Table 6.1. Four agencies have received overall grades of A in managing for results—the Veterans Health Administration (1999), the United States Coast Guard (2000), the National Weather Service (2001), and the United States Postal Service (2001). At the other end of the

Table 6.1. Federal Agency Grades, 1999–2001

Year/Agency	Overall Grade	MFR	FM	HR	IM	PAM
1999						
Customs Service	C	C	B	C	C	*
Environmental Protection Agency	B−	C	B	C	B	B
Federal Aviation Administration	C	B	D	C	C	C
Federal Emergency Management Agency	B	B	B	B	B	C
Federal Housing Administration	B−	C	C	B	B	*
Food and Drug Administration	B	B	B	B	B	*
Food and Nutrition Service	B	B	B	B	A	*
Food Safety and Inspection Service	B	B	B	C	B	*
Health Care Financing Administration	C	C	C	B	D	*
Immigration and Naturalization Service	C−	C	D	D	C	C
Internal Revenue Service	C	B	B	C	D	*
Occupational Safety and Health Administration	B−	C	B	C	B	*
Patent and Trademark Office	B−	B	B	C	C	*
Social Security Administration	A	B	A	A	A	*
Veterans Health Administration	B	A	B	B	B	B
2000						
Army Corps of Engineers	B	B	B	A	B	B
Coast Guard	A	A	B	A	A	A
National Park Service	C	C	C	B	C	C
Office of Student Financial Assistance	C	B	C	C	C	*
Veterans Benefits Administration	B−	B	C	B	C	B

Table 6.1. *Continued*

Year/Agency	Overall Grade	MFR	FM	HR	IM	PAM
2001						
Administration for Children and Families	B	B	B	B	B	*
Bureau of Consular Affairs	C	C	C	C	B	*
Bureau of Indian Affairs	D	D	C	C	D	D
Forest Service	C	C	D	B	C	C
National Aeronautics and Space Administration	B	B	C	B	B	B
National Weather Service	A	A	A	A	A	A
Postal Service	A−	A	A	C	B	A

*No separate grade was given in physical asset management; in these cases agencies had no significant nontechnology assets.

spectrum was the Bureau of Indian Affairs (2001) with a grade of D. In addition to these five, thirteen agencies received B grades in managing for results, while the remaining nine received C grades.

What are the stories and lessons that underlie the grades in managing for results for these agencies? First, the federal government was dominated over three years of our study by the legislative requirements of the Government Performance and Results Act (GPRA). GPRA, which took effect in 1993, requires agencies to engage in strategic planning, performance planning, and performance reporting. Federal agencies have faced the challenge of presenting results information since GPRA required its first performance reports in 1999, The FPP has found that many agencies are doing a good job of complying with GPRA. The exceptions tend to come in two areas.

First, a number of agencies are still having difficulty developing measures of outcomes, preferring to concentrate on outputs. This is understandable. Agencies have control over their outputs, whereas outcomes are often not under their direct control. It is easier for the Social Security Administration to focus on speed and accuracy of checks rather than on elderly poverty. The Customs Service measures the number of pounds of contraband seized as an indicator of the success of its drug interdiction programs, though an equally compelling argument could be made that truly successful drug interdiction would result in no contraband to seize. The Bureau of Indian Affairs uses the number of miles of roads maintained as a measure of the quality of its highway programs without regard to road condition or even eventual utility of the road. Other agencies have made much more progress—the Veterans Health Administration measures patient health outcomes; the Weather Service is focused on timely and accurate weather forecasts.

A particular problem that we uncovered in some agencies was a mismatch between the goals of the organization and the measures that are being used to assess progress toward those goals. So while the goal of the National Aeronautics and Space Administration (NASA) for its Space Science enterprise is "to chart the evolution of the universe from origin to destiny," it quite understandably does not have any performance measures that would allow it to tell how well it is doing. It does have a lot of measures that will tell it about progress in terms of project-level results. This is a typical challenge for a research and development agency.

A perhaps less-explainable example of the same phenomenon was found in the Bureau of Consular Affairs. While there are two goals in the Department of State strategic plan that are primarily under the control of Bureau of Consular Affairs—"to protect the safety and security of American citizens who travel and live abroad" and "to facilitate travel to U.S. by foreign visitors, immigrants, and refugees, while deterring entry by those who threaten or abuse our system"—it does not measure anything that would directly tell it how it is doing. Instead, it focuses on, for example, the waiting times for visas and the percentage of passport applications processed within twenty-five days of receipt. One of the reasons that the Bureau of Consular Affairs does not concentrate more resolutely on results is that it has very little incentive to do so. In the wake of the World Trade Center bombing in 1993, the agency received access to new user-fee revenue specifically earmarked to allow it to hire more staff to process visa applications overseas. The end result of this infusion of new revenue, coupled with attentiveness to the reengineering of work processes, has been to improve services overseas and reduce waiting times for receipt of visas. The agency does not know (or at least cannot prove) that the infusion of resources has actually improved safety. It therefore runs the risk of confusing improvements in work processes and intermediate outcomes with necessarily having improved key mission results in the agency.

Second, focusing on strategic planning and performance measurement in order to comply with provisions of GPRA is hard enough, but the real challenge (unmet in the vast majority of agencies) is to *use* performance information. For many agencies, it is easy to treat GPRA as a set of reporting requirements. GPRA, in fact, is mostly about information, not about the use of that information. Therefore, it is not enough for an agency to say that it is "doing" GPRA well. Good plans or even good results do not imply that an agency is managing for results. The plans may not be used, or management may be satisfied that results are improving without focusing on ensuring that results are as good as they can be. In fact, the best examples that we found of managing for results were cases where the results "culture" had infiltrated the entire agency. At the Veterans Health Administration, for example, performance agreements between the undersecretary and regional directors hold those directors accountable, among other things, for patient health. In the Weather Service, management is organized around the principle of being a "no surprise" service. The challenge is to sustain this momentum. A recent General Accounting Office study cited a falloff in the use of performance information by agencies, suggesting that the momentum created by the establishment of performance measures—even good ones—has not translated into incentives for using those measures in many agencies (GAO, 2001a).

What are the critical success factors underlying successful managing for results?

1. *It is easier to manage for results if everyone agrees on what they want you to do.* Holmes (1996) has said that the key to performance management is "clarity of task and purpose" coupled with authority to manage and accountability of managers for results. Most federal agencies do not operate in an environment where there is anything approaching "clarity of task and purpose." This is probably unavoidable, given the fragmentation of political power envisioned by the framers. But agencies with clearer goals do have an easier time managing for results, because they are not continually redefining what they mean by "results." Thus, we found that the Weather Service or the Social Security Administration would be expected to have an easier time of it than the Forest Service or the Customs Service.

2. *Strong leaders set the tone for managing for results.* If there is no commitment at the top, it is very difficult for agencies to make the kind of sustained commitment to results-based management that is necessary for success. We found several cases where leadership seemed to have made a difference. VHA Undersecretary Ken Kizer and his management team focused resolutely on results from top to bottom, including engaging in performance agreements with top managers; these agreements held them

accountable for patient health outcomes. FEMA Administrator James Lee Witt took an agency that was practically famous for being unresponsive and turned it into a respected partner of states and local governments in dealing with the aftermath of natural disasters. At the National Weather Service, Director Jack Kelly made sure that the agency was focused on outcomes and that they had the tools to do their job by pushing a technology system that had long been languishing.

3. *Having balanced measures, including measures of outcomes is important.* Increasingly, there is evidence that people manage to measures, but that is only a good thing if we are measuring the right things. In 1997 and 1998 the Internal Revenue Service got itself into some famous hot water with the Congress *because* it was focusing on results. Congress had been pushing the IRS for years to maximize the level of revenue that it collected, based on existing tax law. This ultimately led to the IRS's setting collection targets for its agents, which in turn led to these agents behaving somewhat aggressively toward delinquent taxpayers. The problem here was not that the IRS was measuring "dollars collected" as a result. It was that it was failing to balance collections with other kinds of measures, such as measures of public satisfaction. Although it is certainly not the only way to accomplished balanced measurement, some agencies have adopted the "balanced scorecard" approach. For example, the U.S. Postal Service explicitly recognizes three "voices"—the voice of the customer, the voice of the employee, and the voice of the business.

4. *Despite the presence of good performance measures, the lack of good data can be an impediment.* Simply identifying performance measures is not enough. Reliable data need to be collected that will enable agencies to understand how their operations stack up according to those measures. For example, the Centers for Medicare and Medicare Services (CMS), formerly the Health Care Financing Administration (HCFA), must rely on the states that administer the Medicaid program and contractors that administer the Medicare program for data.* CMS, however, has very little in the way of leverage to get those entities to comply. A similar situation exists in the Administration for Children and Families, whose evaluations of Head Start and the Temporary Assistance to Needy Families block grants are hamstrung by reliance on state and local data in evaluating its effectiveness.

5. *Incentives need to be present to actually use performance information for*

---

*In 2001, the Bush administration renamed HCFA, which is now called the Centers for Medicare and Medicaid Services (CMS).

management. Although federal agencies have expended a great deal of time and attention developing measures of outcomes (and much work still needs to be done), the problems of developing those measures pale in comparison to the problems associated with using those measures for decision making. One of the most difficult problems associated with the use of performance information has to do with incentives. In the final analysis, agencies need to be convinced that something that matters to them might actually be affected by performance information. For example, the goal of many advocates of "performance-based budgeting" is for budgetary decisions to be influenced by performance information. This is difficult to carry out in practice. The Congress, for example, does not currently have incentives to pay much attention to performance information in the budget process, focusing instead on inputs, such as which congressional district the funding will flow into. Another place where agencies can make use of performance information is in holding individual managers accountable for achieving outcomes. But this is also quite difficult to do because outcomes are not under the control of agency managers, who are understandably resistant to being held accountable for things they do not control.

Two agencies that we looked at that have made exemplary use of performance information in day-to-day operations are the Veterans' Health Administration and Coast Guard. These cases may be instructive about both the characteristics of successful performance management and the pitfalls that can be faced by agencies in pursuing results-based management.

Veterans Health Administration (VHA). One of the key components of the Department of Veterans Affairs, the VHA has responsibility for operating a nationwide network of veterans hospitals and clinics. In the 1990s, the VHA has been among the most active federal agencies in focusing on results-based management. This began under the direction of Undersecretary Ken Kizer, who started VHA on an aggressive strategic planning effort soon after taking over the agency in 1993. Four components were central to this effort. The first was the development of outcome measures for the agency that enabled it to gauge its success in promoting the health of veterans. Second, the agency engaged in a major reorganization into twenty-two Veterans Integrated Service Networks (VISNs), a regional arrangement that shifted accountability and control from individual hospitals and the central office to these new VISNs. Third, the agency developed performance contracts between the VHA undersecretary and the VISN directors. These performance contracts attempted to hold the directors accountable for, among other things, patient outcomes. Fourth, and perhaps most significant, was the resource allocation formula created by the Veterans Equitable Resource Allocation (VERA) framework. VERA attempts to reallocate resources away from regions that have lost veteran population (largely the Northeast and Midwest) to regions that have been gaining veterans (mostly the South and West). By doing this, VHA attempts to better target its resources toward where its clientele is, as opposed to where its hospitals have been. While congressional opposition to closing hospitals has limited the scope of what VERA has been able to accomplish, it is nonetheless a notable example of an agency directing resources with an eye toward outcomes, in the face of pressure to maintain the status quo. A footnote to the story of VHA is the fate of Undersecretary Kizer himself. While one might think that Kizer would be the poster child for managing for results and would thus be rewarded for his efforts, in fact he had angered some within the Congress so much for attempting to close facilities that he could not be renominated when his four-year term expired in 1998.

United States Coast Guard. The Coast Guard was one of the earliest agencies on the results bandwagon, bringing with it an established commitment to long-term planning. Its Marine Safety program was one of the original pilot programs under GPRA. The Coast Guard provided much of the intellectual impetus and staffing that contributed to the Transportation Department's highly regarded GPRA strategic and performance plans.

The Coast Guard has embraced performance management for two reasons. First, it is continually responding to the need to "do more with less" because Congress routinely adds additional responsibilities without accompanying these responsibilities with adequate funding. Second, as the Coast Guard has no obvious constituency that fights for increased funding on the Hill, it has decided that it may be able to compete for resources if it develops a reputation as an effective user of those resources.

As an example of results-based management in the Coast Guard, the Marine Safety program has changed its focus from measuring response to potential nautical disasters to trying to prevent these disasters from occurring in the first place. This means that the prevention of marine accidents (and thus the protection of life and property) has been a key performance measurement focus. The Coast Guard has made one of the most successful linkages of any agency between planning and budgeting. Its algorithm for relating performance and the budget is represented by the following formula: "Desired outcome determines needed capability determines required resources." Strategic and performance plans are built from the ground up, and all budget requests much be justified in terms of their contribution to the meeting of planned objectives.* The Coast Guard is also a leader in integrated management. It was one of the first agencies to follow the guidance represented in the OMB's Capital Programming Guide, which advocates strategic physical asset management that ties the acquisition and maintenance of physical assets to their contribution to mission success. Similar stories could be told in human resources management and management of technology.

Human Resources Management (HR)

For human resources management, the project has focused on the acquisition and deployment of personnel consistent with the strategic vision of agencies. Human resources management is crucial to the ability of federal agencies to achieve results for two main reasons. First, approximately two-thirds of most agency budgets consist of personnel costs. Second, the federal government currently faces what the GAO refers to as a "human capital crisis" because a significant percentage of the federal workforce will be eligible to retire within the next five years. This will create challenges of recruiting new employees, planning for the succession of existing employees, and ensuring that employees are deployed when and where needed.

The criteria that we have used to examine human resource management focused on several key areas:

- Whether the agency has sufficient people, with the appropriate skills and abilities, to fulfill mission requirements;
- Workforce planning, which includes the development of a strategic vision for the future concerning what employees will be necessary and where they will need to be located;
- The ability to locate employees where they will be needed in order to achieve the strategic results being pursued by the agency;
- Providing managers the flexibility to manage employees, including hiring, reward, and discipline.

Over the three years of the FPP thus far, the average grade for human resources management has been slightly below that for managing for results,

---

*It is worth noting that this linkage between planning and budgeting seems to work quite well in the budget formulation and execution stages of the budget process, but has worked less well during OMB and congressional consideration of the budget.

but nonetheless it is approximately a B— overall. Again, however, this masks a great deal of variation. Over the three years, sixteen agencies received grades of A or B, while the remaining eleven agencies received C and D grades. Four agencies received overall A grades: the Social Security Administration (1999), the U.S. Coast Guard (2000), the Army Corps of Engineers (2000), and the National Weather Service (2001). Only one agency—the Immigration and Naturalization Service (1999)—received an overall grade of D. The remaining twenty-two agencies were evenly split between B and C grades.

Perhaps the most important lesson that emerged from our review of human resources management concerned its relationship to a larger management vision in federal agencies. The GAO has been a leader in attempting to get federal agencies to focus on "human capital" as a part of their larger strategic vision. A "self-assessment" framework published in 1999 by GAO encourages agencies to create organizational alignment within a broader strategic vision; to foster commitment leadership through workforce and succession planning; to recruit, hire, and develop appropriately skilled staff; and to promote accountability and motivation for employees to assist agencies in achieving results (GAO, 2000).

In the course of establishing a vision for human resources management in federal agencies, the GAO has done research to uncover common themes in successful management of human capital in the private sector. Many of these criteria are strikingly similar to those employed by the FPP in evaluating successful federal agencies practices, including: the integration of human capital concerns into a larger strategic vision for the corporation; sustaining leadership within the organization; identifying the key competencies necessary for achieving mission success, and hiring and training accordingly; and holding employees accountable for achieving results, in part through the use of financial and other incentives (GAO, 2000).

Many of the agencies that were graded the highest in human resources management exhibited characteristics consistent with the ideals presented above. They engaged in workforce planning and held employees increasingly accountable for results. But the general findings of the FPP indicate that there are several past and future challenges in human resources management. How these challenges are met will largely determine the success that federal agencies will have in the future.

1. *Success in workforce planning will be essential as agencies prepare for potential imbalances between skills and future workforce needs.* Current estimates are that by 2004 nearly one-third of the federal workforce will be

eligible to retire and another 21 percent will be eligible for early retirement. These potential shortfalls in personnel will come on the heels of the aggressive downsizing that took place during the Clinton administration, when government reinvention efforts occurred somewhat haphazardly and buyouts were offered indiscriminately without accounting for whether remaining employees would have the necessary skills. This clearly is a cry for workforce planning, but in many agencies this is a luxury, taking a back seat to just making things happen on a day-to-day basis. In NASA, for example, there is recognition that attention needs to be paid to long-term workforce needs, but the agency has strong incentives to focus on near-term problems and to ignore the necessary planning that would address potential skill imbalances three or five years in the future.

2. *Many agencies suffered self-inflicted wounds from engaging in overly aggressive or ill- conceived downsizing efforts.* The Clinton administration, partially in an effort to demonstrate its antipathy to "big government," engaged in a relatively aggressive downsizing effort.* For example, Vice-President Al Gore's National Performance Review promoted the elimination of almost 300,000 "middle management" positions in federal agencies. Some agencies heard the message a little too clearly. For example, the Coast Guard cut approximately four thousand jobs between 1994 and 1998. Current Coast Guard leaders are convinced that the agency approached streamlining a bit too zealously and that this has inhibited the agency by costing it in terms of core capacities. According to a March 2000 article, then-director of resources Rear Admiral David Nicholson argued, "We cut back recruiting, let people who wanted to go leave. There was no thought to middle management capacities. . . . We have found we hurt ourselves a lot" (Laurent, 2000: 43). And the Coast Guard is not alone. In the wake of welfare reform, the Administration for Children and Families (ACF) reduced staff from 2,200 in 1993 to 1,500 in 2001. Although this was understandable given the scaling back of the ACF mission, the staff that were left did not necessarily have the skills necessary to match the remaining mission requirements.

3. *Some agencies have embraced labor-management partnerships, while others have very poor relations between unions and managers.* Particularly in agencies where many employees are unionized, the quality of labor-manage-

---

*This is true at least in terms of federal employees. Some observers, such as Paul Light (1999), note that the effect of this downsizing may have been to shift service delivery from federal employees to contractors.

ment relations can affect the ability of agencies to accomplish core tasks. In the Internal Revenue Service, for example, the National Treasury Employees Union (NTEU) was given a specific "place at the table" in the reformed IRS management structure. On the other hand, difficult relations between the Patent and Trademark Office and (in particular) its patent union hampered management efforts to move into revamped space and to become a performance-based organization. A subsequent change in leadership of the agency in the last two years of the Clinton administration is credited with improving relations with unions, which have dropped opposition to both of these changes. The U.S. Postal Service is also hampered by poor relations with its unions. This is particularly significant because unions represent 700,000 of the Postal Service's approximately 800,000 employees. The Postal Service labor problems are caused, in part, by an extraordinary backlog of more than 126,000 grievances as of 2000. In fact, the sheer number of Postal Service grievances is itself an indicator of poor relations. In 1999, 6,300 grievances went to arbitration; by comparison, in the entire auto industry, with 400,000 unionized employees, only 11 grievances went to arbitration in 1998. These poor relationships have real impacts on the ability of the Postal Service to be efficient and responsive. The Postal Service is unable to reduce positions in areas where workload is declining because it cannot get the unions to agree to shifting positions from lower-volume areas to higher-volume areas.

4. *The federal government has difficulty recruiting and retaining employees, particularly for positions requiring technical and scientific skills.* Especially in agencies that rely on staff with scientific or technical training, the federal government cannot keep up with the salaries and benefits provided by private sector competitors. NASA is perhaps the best example from the twenty-seven agencies studied by the FPP. As in the Coast Guard, the NASA downsizing effort left the agency with skill gaps in key areas. But NASA arguably has more barriers to recruitment than does the Coast Guard; it also has been granted special pay authority to offset some of these barriers. Presumably, the private sector dislocations in the dot-com industry will increase the supply of technological personnel available to federal agencies.

On the other hand, the National Weather Service (NWS) has virtually no recruitment and retention problems. Not only is it the employer of choice for young meteorologists, but they stay. The average tenure among the managers returning our FPP managers' survey was twenty years, higher by five years than the average tenure among all seven of the 2001 FPP agencies.

Furthermore, NWS employees actually welcome transfers between different facilities because they enjoy the challenges inherent in experiencing different climatic conditions.

5. *The federal government in general has embraced a number of changes designed to boost morale, such as flexible schedules and work locations and reward programs for high-performing employees.* Many federal agencies are increasingly recognizing that the creation of a "family-friendly" work environment is important. For example, under the leadership of former Secretary Donna Shalala, the Department of Health and Human Services (HHS) focused on a "work-life" initiative that embraced flextime and flexiplace. The HHS agencies that we reviewed, such as the Food and Drug Administration (FDA) and the Health Care Financing Administration, had seen real gains in morale resulting from this program. In a 1998 survey of FDA employees, 84 percent said that they almost always or usually were able to balance work and family life through the use of flexible schedules and leave options.

Agencies have also increasingly turned to awards programs where employees or groups are able to be rewarded for achieving excellent results. For example, one of the added benefits of the performance-based organization status for the Education Department's Office of Student Financial Assistance is that executives can be offered salaries and bonuses up to the maximum Senior Executive Service pay rate in exchange for performance contracts with measurable goals. Other agencies have also embraced performance awards in a more limited way.

Financial Management (FM)

Federal financial management has received substantial attention over the past decade. Starting with the passage of the Chief Financial Officers' Act in 1990, federal agencies have been under pressure to improve their accounting systems and management of financial resources. Several other laws, including the Federal Management Reform Act of 1994 and the Federal Acquisition Reform Act of 1996 have also sought to improve agency management. In addition, agencies have found that the new emphasis on performance management has carried with it a concern for the financial tools necessary for effective results-based administration, including an attention to the true costs of programs (including indirect costs) and the provision of appropriate flexibility for federal agencies in managing resources. Accordingly, the issues focused on by the project in evaluating financial management systems have included the following:

- Provision of timely and accurate data on financial resources to managers where and when needed, a major challenge for many agencies that have had difficulty developing integrated financial management systems.
- Progress in developing cost accounting systems, in order to be able to get a better handle on the true cost of delivering services, is essential to being able to link performance and the budget.
- A linkage of planning and budgeting systems, as opposed to a regime where strategic and performance planning and budget planning and implementation operate as if they are independent of each other, is desirable if the budget is to become more informed by performance considerations.
- The development of financial statements that can generate unqualified audit opinions is considered a leading indicator of financial management performance and is related to the ability to provide accurate information in addition to being indicative of good stewardship of federal resources.
- Providing managers appropriate flexibility to manage resources, as opposed to having *ex ante* spending controls that exist for their own sake, assists in managing for performance, provided these flexibilities are coupled with accountability for results.

Over the three years of the project, the average grade for financial management was somewhat lower than for the previous two categories, approaching a C+ overall. Once again, this average masks substantial variation. While sixteen agencies received A's or B's, eleven agencies were in the C or D category. Only three agencies over the three years had A grades—the Social Security Administration (1999), the National Weather Service (2001), and the U.S. Postal Service (2001). On the other hand, three agencies—the Immigration and Naturalization Service (1999), the Federal Aviation Administration (1999), and the Forest Service (2001)—received D grades. Of the remaining twenty-one agencies, there were thirteen B grades and eight C grades.

Across the federal government, there have been a number of crosscutting financial management issues that have tended to impede federal agency progress. Consistent with its own mission, the GAO has been at the forefront in identifying these shortcomings. On a government-wide level, the GAO reports that the federal government cannot account for billions of dollars of property and equipment, estimate the cost of most federal credit and loan programs, determine the proper amount of certain contingent liabilities, estimate environmental liability, and guarantee that disbursements are property recorded (McIntire-Peters, 2000).

The FPP has highlighted a number of specific financial management results:

1. *Cost accounting has been somewhat slow in catching on in federal agencies.* Agencies have found it particularly difficult to capture indirect costs—so-called overhead costs associated with budget, personnel, or information systems, for example. Without capturing these costs, it is quite difficult for agencies to determine the true costs of delivering services, and thus it is difficult to compare these costs across programs. Progress in developing cost accounting systems has been more rapid in agencies that rely heavily on user fees for operations, largely because establishing an appropriate fee structure has necessitated attention to the true costs of doing business. For example, the Patent and Trademark Office (PTO) relies exclusively on application fees for its revenues. This has forced the agency to invest substantial resources in developing a cost accounting system to enable it to justify its fee schedule. Using activity-based costing, the PTO demonstrated to the Congress that patent fees were higher than could be justified by costs, while trademark fees were lower than costs (Friel, 2000).

The reliance on user fees for an increasing level of financial resources carries with it mixed incentives for some agencies. An agency that is financed through fees may find it necessary to be more responsive to those who are paying the freight than it is to the general public. Take, as an example, the Food and Drug Administration. Since 1992 the FDA has received a substantial percentage of its budget for reviewing drug applications (40% as of 1997) from a user fee paid by applicant pharmaceutical companies. This fee was reauthorized in 1997 only after substantial negotiations between the FDA and the pharmaceutical industry over what could and could not be financed using the fees. For example, the companies insisted that the FDA not use any of the user-fee money to finance basic research, even though the FDA believes basic research is necessary in order to effectively review applications. In particular, the FDA has been forced to embrace a performance-measurement framework that puts heavy emphasis on the speed of action on drug applications rather than on issues related to promoting public health. While the FDA argues that getting drugs to market faster promotes public health in the vast majority of cases, it does not do so in any case where a problem drug is approved too quickly because not enough research was done concerning potential harmful effects. As federal agencies continue to explore more and more user fees to finance services, it is useful to consider the extent to which these fees establish potentially counterproductive incentives for these agencies.*

2. *Many agencies still need to make substantial progress in order to assure that their financial systems provide timely and accurate information to managers.* The federal government has a history of woefully inadequate financial management systems. One particular and longstanding problem has to do with the interoperability of these systems—that is, whether systems "talk" to each other in an integrated way. A number of federal agencies have reported that they need to access a number of systems in order to generate basic accounting data. Managers in some agencies are unable to access even basic information on funds spent and available for spending. In other agencies, data are available at the field level but not at the central office level. For example, we found that in both the National Park Service and the U.S. Forest Service managers in the field had established financial systems that enabled them to know what they had available and to manage day-to-day activities in a given park or forest, but since these systems do not talk to each other, they are limited in their ability to provide enterprise-level data. Considerable money has been spent over the years in trying to establish better financial systems in agencies. NASA has already implemented two failed systems and is hoping that their third attempt will be more successful. NASA runs nine separate finance and accounting systems, and only through "heroic" work on the part of finance and accounting personnel who reconcile data manually has NASA has been able to generate clean audit opinions six years in a row (McIntire-Peters, 2001: 18).

3. *The federal government as a whole has made substantial progress in generating unqualified audit opinions since the passage of the Chief Financial Officers Act.* Many agencies that we looked at have been able to generate "clean" audit opinions, including the Postal Service, NASA, the IRS, and the Social Security Administration. In fact, all twenty-four of the agencies covered by the CFO Act met the March 1, 2001, deadline for turning in audited financial statements, and eighteen of those received clean opinions (up from fifteen the year before). Notably, given the discussion of financial systems above, some of these agencies (see the NASA example) have only been able

---

*See "Drug Money." *Government Executive* 1999, 31(2): 53–56 for more information on the relationship between FDA and the pharmaceutical industry.

to generate clean opinions after expending much time and money manually posting transactions. This puts agencies at risk of not being able to sustain this positive momentum in the future. At the same time, there are still a substantial number of agencies that have been unable to generate clean audits. In some of these cases, such as the Health Care Financing Administration, the agencies have generated qualified opinions. The most serious cases are agencies such as the Forest Service, the INS, and the Federal Aviation Administration, which had disclaimers of opinion at the time that we reviewed them. Getting clean audits is not just about keeping books, but about giving good, reliable, and timely information to managers. In that sense, financial management and information management systems fit together. If you don't know how much you have spent and how much you have remaining, good management is difficult.

4. *Finally, limited progress has been made in terms of linking planning and budgeting systems.* Agencies where this linkage has been made are the exception rather than the rule. The Coast Guard, as noted above, stands out as an example of an agency that has paid particular attention to this linkage. The VERA system in VHA is another clear example of a system where resource allocation in clearly linked to the mission goals of the agency. It is still the rule, at least for the agencies that we reviewed, for planning staffs and budget staffs to operate independently of each other, and for compliance with GPRA directives for performance and strategic planning to not link directly to acquisition or management of resources.

Information Management (IM)

Information management is not just about computers but often is discussed and evaluated as if it is. In part, this has to do with the perception that technology and information are synonymous. While effective information can be generated by technological means, spending money on technology for its own sake is not necessarily a good investment. The approach of the FPP has been to focus on having the right information get to the right people when they need it to do their jobs.

The criteria used to evaluate information management are consistent with this focus and address the following questions:

1. Do managers have timely and accurate information necessary to carry out the mission of the agency, and does the agency have the capacity to determine the extent to which they have this information?

2. To what extent does the agency understand the relationship between the procurement of additional information resources and the achievement of results?
3. Does information about agency operations and performance flow internally within the agency and to external stakeholders?
4. Does the agency use electronic means to deliver services and communicate with the public?

Over the three years of the project, the average grade for information management was a B−. Of the twenty-seven agencies evaluated, sixteen of them received grades of A or B, while eleven received C or D grades. Four agencies—the Food and Nutrition Service, the Social Security Administration, the Coast Guard, and the National Weather Service—received A grades, while three agencies—the Internal Revenue Service, the Health Care Financing Administration, and the Bureau of Indian Affairs—received D's. On the remaining twenty agencies, eleven received B grades, while the remaining nine received grades of C.

The most important characteristic of agencies that were successful in information management was having an integrated approach. In these agencies, the management of information is an integral part of managing for results. For example, Veterans Benefits Administration managers, from Undersecretary Joseph Thompson, to regional directors, to line workers, were able to access information on agency results at the click of a computer mouse. In order to get there, however, the VBA needed to figure out ways to integrate data from different computer systems in a way that it could be presented in a useable manner (Ferris, 2000: 28). This concern for integration is an indicator of the movement in the federal government toward strategic management of technology.

1. *The Clinger-Cohen Act has been an important development in terms of getting agencies to look at information technology (IT) investments as they relate to mission success.* This act, which became law in 1996, requires agencies to pursue process improvements before pursing technological solutions, to evaluate IT investments in terms of their value added to mission success, to develop performance measures to relate IT success to broader management concerns, and to report annually to the OMB on the progress made in IT investments. But saying this is not the same thing as doing it. Coming up with performance measures for information technology can prove particularly challenging.

2. *Dealing with the Y2K bug provided additional resources for technology*

but diverted some agencies from making additional progress in favor of "keeping the doors open." At the same time that Clinger-Cohen was mandating these new requirements, most federal agencies found themselves facing a much more immediate concern—rendering their technology systems immune from potential "Y2K" computer disaster. This problem, caused by the potential that agency IT systems would recognize the year 2000 as 1900 therefore causing dislocations in benefit processing and other crucial government services, hijacked resources in many agencies that might have been devoted to getting a better handle on performance measurement. The Y2K problem, conversely, encouraged resources to be devoted to modernization in some agencies when these resources might otherwise not have been forthcoming. Some agencies, such as the Social Security Administration, had been at the forefront of Y2K readiness, starting the conversion process more than ten years in advance of the year 2000. Others found themselves scrambling to bring their systems into compliance before the day of reckoning arrived. In the end, virtually all federal computer systems passed the Y2K test with flying colors, largely due to advance planning and substantial resource investments.

3. *Unsuccessful systems modernizations can waste valuable time and money; successful reforms can provide major support for agencies in achieving mission success.* In spite of this success, examples abound, in the limited number of agencies that we looked at, of very expensive technology mistakes. Probably the best examples among FPP agencies are the Internal Revenue Service (IRS) and the Health Care Financing Administration (HCFA). In the IRS, a Tax Systems Modernization effort was scrapped in 1997 after $3.4 billion had already been spent on it; IRS had nothing to show for this substantial investment. While it pales in scope to the IRS debacle, HCFA put an $80 million Medicare Transactions System on the shelf after a three-and-a-half-year attempt to bring it on line. Over that time, the total cost estimate for the system had skyrocketed from $151 million to more than $1 billion. In both of these cases, agencies were criticized for inattentiveness up front to understanding the core mission requirements that such a system would be designed to address.

On the other hand, when technology systems are considered as an integral part of achieving mission success, the results are much more satisfying. Take, as a case in point, the Advanced Weather Interactive Processing System (AWIPS), which the National Weather Service has had in development for more than ten years. By 1996 the price tag of the system rose from $350 million to $525 million, and an IRS- or HCFA-like disaster appeared on the horizon. New NWS director Jack Kelly, who took over the agency in 1998, put one person in charge of the system and established a goal of finishing it by June 1999 at a cost of no more than $550 million. Today AWIPS is online and providing just the kind of weather information that it was designed to provide. In fact, the NWS claims that the documented improvements in warning times and accuracy that have been achieved are a direct result of systems modernization.

4. *One of the key lessons is that increasingly management of technology means management of contractors providing technology services.* One of the biggest challenges facing managers of technology systems is holding contractors accountable for delivering products. Information technology management also includes contract management, which is a big challenge in many agencies. For example, NASA must, in order to achieve success in its missions, manage a disparate set of contractors that must talk to NASA project managers and to each other. In the past, the failure to ensure effective communication has compromised some missions, including (most tragically) the 1986 Challenger mission (Romzek and Dubnick, 1987). More recently, the unsuccessful Mars probe was plagued by communication problems. The challenges of contract management has led many agencies to develop performance-based contracts for technology in an attempt to ensure the delivery of necessary components of modernized systems.

5. *One of the key information management challenges in far-flung federal agencies is the sharing of information both vertically and horizontally across the agency.* Many federal agencies are very spread out, both geographically and organizationally. Nonetheless, it is often important that they share information in order to achieve results. Moreover, it can be important to managers at the top of the agency to have information from agency subunits in order to understand which programs or offices are working effectively and which may have some challenges. In the National Weather Service, the sharing of information between offices and regions is crucial to storm tracking, for example; one of the most important characteristics of the AWIPS system is that it facilitates this information sharing. On the other hand, the Bureau of Indian Affairs central office staff can only compile nationwide data through a Byzantine process potentially involving hundreds of faxes and/or phone calls. Similar information sharing challenges exist in the Forest Service and the Park Service.

Physical Asset Management (PAM)

Many federal agencies do not own substantial physical assets except for computer systems. For this reason, only a little more than half of the agencies evaluated as part of the FPP were even reviewed in terms of their management of physical assets. For those that do have non-IT assets, however, decisions about them are critical to achieving mission success. An agency like the Coast Guard literally cannot survive without its ships and planes; similarly, NASA cannot fulfill its mission adequately without planning for and maintaining assets such as the space shuttle.

Recognizing the importance of planning for capital assets as connected to broader mission requirements, the OMB has issued a Capital Programming Guide, which it proposes that federal agencies use in planning for the acquisition and maintenance of capital assets. In this capital guide, agencies are expected to inform their potential acquisition of assets by asking "three pesky questions":

1. Does the investment in a major capital asset support core or priority mission functions that need to be performed by the federal government?
2. Does the investment need to be undertaken by the requesting agency because no alternative private sector or governmental source can better support the function?
3. Does the investment support work processes that have been simplified or otherwise redesigned to reduce costs, improve effectiveness, and make maximum use of commercial off-the-shelf technology?

The most important feature of the capital programming guide is that is discourages agencies from thinking about capital as a "wish list" that is disconnected from basic questions about what the agency needs to accomplish. Under the regime advocated by OMB, there should be a direct connection between the priorities of the agency as identified in the GPRA strategic and performance plans, and the management of physical assets. Consistent with this regime, the factors used by the FPP in evaluating federal agencies' physical asset management performance include:

- The existence of sufficient equipment and facilities, able to be deployed in the right places at the right time to enable the agency to carry out its mission;

- A process for acquiring and maintaining physical assets that is clearly related to how those assets will contribute to mission success, as articulated by the OMB capital programming guide or some similar guidance;
- The ability of the agency to track the condition of its facilities and to understand what an appropriate acquisition, replacement, and maintenance schedule would be.

While physical asset management was only evaluated separately in fourteen of the twenty-seven FPP agencies, it tends to be critically important to mission success in those agencies. In the VHA, or NASA, or the Coast Guard, it is difficult to imagine how the agency could effectively achieve its mission without appropriate management of physical assets. Of the fourteen agencies evaluated for physical asset management, three—the Coast Guard, the Postal Service, and the Weather Service—received A grades. At the other end of the spectrum, the Bureau of Indian Affairs received the lone D grade. In addition to these, there were five B grades—EPA, VHA, VBA, NASA, and the Army Corps. The five remaining agencies—the Park Service, the Forest Service, FEMA, FAA, and INS—received C grades.

Several lessons emerged from our review of physical asset management in these agencies:

1. *Clearly the factor that most sets the well-managed agencies apart is their attentiveness to the mission implications of their capital acquisition and maintenance.* In the Coast Guard, which is widely viewed as having the most sophisticated capital management process among federal agencies, the capital management plan is fully integrated into a broader results-oriented management framework. If the Coast Guard has a goal of minimizing death, injury, or property damage, the question that it addresses concerns how its capital assets can assist it in meeting that objective at the least cost. For example, an older ship might be able to do the job, but it may also require more maintenance, which has both financial costs and operational costs in terms of downtime. The agency focuses not just on the useful life of an asset, with replacement coming on a fixed schedule, but on total ownership cost, which includes both the cost of acquiring and the cost of maintaining. Spending more money up front may sometimes reduce costs. The Coast Guard has also focused on holding procurement contractors to both cost and performance goals.

2. *Maintenance is chronically underfunded in many agencies, largely because members of Congress have incentives to build things but not to maintain*

them. Agency after agency told stories of the facilities that they had been provided or prevented from closing by the Congress. For example, the VHA has chronic difficulties in closing hospitals, even in areas where veteran populations have shrunk substantially. But while getting money to keep hospitals operating is not a problem, getting money to maintain aging facilities is another story entirely. The only agency that we uncovered that did an effective job of maintaining existing physical assets was the Postal Service, in large part because the Congress does not micromanage its maintenance funding process.* At the Forest Service, deferred maintenance has reportedly resulted in maintenance backlogs of more than $16 billion in roads and bridges, buildings, recreation sites, and trails. The National Park Service estimates its maintenance backlog exceeds $5 billion.

3. *Contributing to the difficulty of maintaining capital in many agencies are chronic problems in maintaining physical asset inventories.* On the other hand, it is difficult to determine what condition your facilities and equipment are in, and therefore accurately determine maintenance needs, if you do not have a thorough inventory of assets. Several agencies evaluated in the FPP, including both the Forest Service and the Bureau of Indian Affairs, do not have adequate inventories of assets.

Conclusion

In this chapter we have attempted to review three years of findings about federal agency management. This effort has necessarily focused to this point on findings by management area. It is important to keep in mind, however, that management, as we consider it in this project, is not simply a listing of results by issue areas or "best practices" that can be taken from one agency and tried in another. Management is about integrating these management systems toward some common end. The National Weather Service and the Coast Guard, for example, are exemplary federal agencies not only because they do so many things well but also because they manage toward a common set of goals. Next, therefore, we will turn to a larger set of lessons about managing in the public sector, one that is informed by our findings of state and local management and federal management as presented in Chapters 5 and 6.

*It is worth noting that even in the Postal Service the recent disagreements about postal revenues have led to a cutback in capital construction and maintenance. The effectiveness of the capital planning process, however, contributed to a relatively smooth process through which the agency was able to trim $1 billion from its proposed $3.6 billion 2001 capital improvement budget.

7 | The Big Lessons

As the previous two chapters suggest, the data and findings generated by the Government Performance Project (GPP) and the Federal Performance Project (FPP) are extensive and complex. Each level and type of government analyzed revealed lessons and practices best explained by that government's size, structure, or function. At the same time, the lessons of the GPP and FPP taken together lead to broad insights and conclusions about effective management in public organizations.

The first significant lesson is that *management does indeed matter.* Good management has different effects on, and follows different paths to, performance in different organizations and levels of government. Without any question, however, the quality of management in government organizations is an important factor in the ability of those organizations to effectively pursue their mission and to use resources well. Good management matters in stable as well as turbulent times; it is a significant influence on the organization's ability to maintain an effective course.

The role played by management is closely intertwined with that of leadership. In every effective public organization we studied, at whatever level of government, a readily identifiable and strong leader or team of leaders was responsible for providing energy and direction. Those leaders were elected officials, political appointees, career civil servants, and teams composed of all of these. But in each government with the capacity for high performance, there was a powerful leadership influence. In those governments and government agencies found to lack capacity, the absence of direction and leadership was notable.

While leadership appears to be a contributor to good management, it is not a *sufficient* condition for capacity for performance. Good leaders may find themselves hamstrung, for example, by externally imposed constraints, shifting resources, or multiple and conflicting missions. Good leadership can be a stimulus for better performance; it can also be the glue that binds and integrates existing systems. Absent basic external support and fundamental internal systemic support, however, even excellent leadership can be a wasted resource.

As hard as these conditions may be to achieve in public organizations, a second set of lessons clearly demonstrates that for public organizations *clarity of purpose and the ability to limit priorities, to carefully align resources with priorities, and to measure progress are strongly associated with management capacity and quality.* It is common practice for legislatures, elected officials, and citizens to have multiple and sometimes conflicting expectations for government programs and performance. Unfortunately, those many expectations are often incorporated into the legislation that formally establishes mission, purpose, and programs for government agencies. These broad missions are rarely—if ever—cut back, even though resources may be. The "mission growing; resources shrinking" syndrome is an increasingly common aspect of government operations and management and was present in a large majority of the governments we studied. In addition, where legislation is left vague (or is contradictory), public agencies are left to "fill in the details," putting them in the unenviable position of being second-guessed after the fact by legislators and others.

In governments with strong capacity, leaders and managers had found ways to limit "mission creep" or to choose and prioritize strategic objectives from the panoply afforded by formal mission statements. Integration of management systems—or at least coordination between them whenever possible—is an important facilitator in this activity. On the flip side, governments and agencies that have not been successful in meeting mission or staying within budget have frequently not targeted activities and have not been successful in linking organizational objectives to organizational activities. They are, sadly, often the beneficiaries of another common public syndrome—rewarding failure—when they are given additional funds to try again. GPP and FPP evidence demonstrates the great likelihood that this unfortunate "failure is its own reward" syndrome becomes a serious spiraling decline without new leadership and sharply different direction.

Two kinds of policy lessons emerge from the GPP and the FPP, and between them, they may provide the most significant lessons of all. First, there is very good evidence that *management systems are important policy and performance variables in their own right.* Effective human resources management, financial management, capital management, and information management systems are critical to the effective targeting of resources and to the matching of resources with strategic objectives. Capable management systems are the tools public leaders need to deliver the services and benefits that citizens have been promised. Although we did not explicitly test causal relationships between capacity and policy outcomes, our data strongly suggest that an organization that does not have the right people or physical assets to do its job is not likely to succeed. An organization that does not know how much money it has or how much of it has been spent is not likely to be blazing a performance path. An agency that cannot provide the appropriate information to top management or line managers when they need to make decisions is not in a good position to deliver results. The ability to create more effective systems and to find the right people to lead them is something that can be changed and manipulated as part of the public policy process. Even civil service systems are not cast in stone, as the experience of some states demonstrates. One state—Georgia—completely scrapped its civil service system and started fresh; another state—Florida—is following suit. It is important, therefore, to view management systems in real policy terms: reforms to them are not "green eye-shade" activities. Management reforms are strongly related to the ability of governments and their agencies to perform well and therefore to the overall quality of government. Changing management systems can change government.

That leads to the other very important policy lesson: that *the story of management reform in U.S. governments is not one of constant failure* or even of too much too often (Light, 1997; Thompson, 2000). Rather, our analyses have demonstrated that management reform is a long-term building of the competencies and components necessary to effective change. We recognize that building long-term capacity is different from shorter term, dramatically obvious change, and we do not suggest that the governments and agencies we studied demonstrated the ability to "turn on a dime." Most governments cannot—and probably should not—do that.

Rather, we suggest that reform is a complicated and lengthy process for public organizations no matter what the government structure or setting. For example, results-based management has long been a goal of reform at all levels of government; nonetheless, we found many examples—even in those governments or agencies with a long and relatively successful history of reforms—of renewed efforts to improve. Human resources management systems in the states demonstrate swings from centralized to decentralized and now to "strategically balanced." The early reforms were not failures; they were an important part of getting reform right. These learning curves are critical to public organizations, engaged as they are in the delicate—and very open—balancing required to satisfy multiple audiences. Moreover, early reforms can create capacity—physical and intellectual—necessary for later efforts to succeed. A longer-term, more comprehensive perspective in assessing the accumulated impact of reform is critical to understanding its real meaning. Does this mean that management system change is without problems or that there are no failures? Of course not. But it does mean that improved understanding of the building blocks and the leadership necessary for effective change is very important.

The final broad lesson is related to this learning. The criteria-based analysis employed by the GPP and the FPP allowed clear and transparent discussion and debate about both the criteria and their application. The governments that were graded also participated extensively in analyzing the effectiveness and accuracy of the criteria. Completion of the lengthy surveys proved to be another kind of learning process for many of the governments involved. In this setting, *the GPP/FPP grades were frequently motivators for change.* Many governments observed that external assessments can be useful guides; the GPP/FPP process, necessitating as it did governments' own intensive participation in the process, facilitated learning not only within the organization but also among governments and agencies and stimulated change in many cases. These changes occurred across the scope of the grades: governments receiving high grades, such as Virginia and Phoenix, wished to do even better and looked to other high performers. Governments and agencies that did not do so well—Alabama is one example—looked to higher-performing governments and agencies for lessons in better management.

Each of these points requires additional discussion and clarification. The remainder of this chapter discusses each in turn and provides examples from the governments studied in the first three years of the project.

Management Matters

Just as common sense suggests that it is best to obtain value for money spent rather than wasting it, good management is preferable to bad or ineffective management. From our findings, it is reasonable to conclude that management can make a difference and that the difference can be either positive or negative. Furthermore, management competence can and does vary not only across governments but within governments as well. As we noted earlier in the book, only rarely did governments and agencies do well or poorly in all of the systems we studied. More commonly, there was strength in some of the systems but room for improvement in others. In addition, we found that management operated differently in different settings and environments.

In particular, it appears that the way management makes a difference varies, depending on the stability of the organization or policy area being managed. We would draw a distinction between managing in a stable environment versus a more turbulent environment. A stable environment is characterized by a relatively high level of consensus about what a government or agency should accomplish as well as a fairly consistent level of the resources necessary to carry out that mission. In such an environment, leaders and employees are more likely to have rather clear direction concerning expectations. In a turbulent environment, the organization is consistently being second-guessed; expectations may be highly variable both within the organization and from the outside; and resource levels are, at best, unstable.

Managing in Stable Settings

Although rescuing an organization in distress may be very dramatic, keeping an organization on track and nimble in stable times is equally important and just as hard. Getting the daily business of government right is an enormous feat. This is not to suggest that managing in stable settings is challenge-free, but only that the bases from which to address the challenges have been carefully constructed. Governments and agencies that managed well in relatively stable times generally did well in several of the systems assessed by the GPP/FPP. They had strengths across the board.

Still, the challenges were daunting. Cities such as Phoenix and Austin confront rapid growth, transportation problems, and environmental issues. They are able to address these problems more strategically and effectively because the "everyday business" of the city is well managed. The same is true of state governments such as Virginia, Washington, and Michigan. Each faces particular urban and economic problems as well as specific resource issues. In each case, again, the leadership and management team has assembled a foundation of effective management and proceeded from that base to address emergent problems. At the federal level, the Social Security Administration, the National Weather Service, and the Coast Guard represent agencies whose management base allows the flexibility and creativity required for problem solving. The Social Security Administration, where effective meeting of mission is crucial to millions of Americans, struggled with some internal coordination problems, but the core ability to process social security payments was not disrupted. The Coast Guard, with limited resources, recruiting challenges, and a wide-ranging set of missions, relies on superb professionalism and managerial talent to retain focus and allocate the resources that are available.

Managing in a Turbulent Environment

Some level of turbulence is essentially a given for public organizations. Nonetheless, some governments and their agencies encounter economic and political settings so disturbed that the first order of business is doing whatever is necessary to calm the change. In these settings, management appears to take on a different role and purpose. Our evidence suggests that in relative stability good management sets the foundation for effective and efficient performance in meeting core tasks and provides leadership with the "cushion" necessary for new strategies and actions to meet nonroutine or emergent challenges. In a turbulent setting, management (and leadership) provide the direction and expertise necessary to weather the storm. They do so by providing clear priorities and parameters for action but also by constant communication of strategy and purpose. Absent such a unifying force or influence, the organization would likely have little ability to pull itself together and move ahead.

The cities of Indianapolis and Washington, D.C., provide examples of cities that, confronted by enormous need for change, responded to the challenge in well-led managerial ways. Although generally the governments in this category showed strength in two or three but not all systems, neither of these cities exactly fits that mode. In the course of economic rebuilding, Indianapolis relied very strongly on budgetary systems and managing for results, and it put excellent systems in place for both; other management systems did not receive such high priority but were still above average in many respects. Washington, D.C., in the hands of a Control Board for many years, essentially needed to rebuild all systems from scratch. It did so with a heavy reliance on financial management and information management. Other systems remained problematic while core strength was rebuilt in targeted systems.

Although many state budgets were seriously affected by the economic downturn in the years following our analysis, at the time of the GPP studies most were still doing relatively well. North Carolina, suffering the impact of floods and hurricanes and realizing earlier than most states that more difficult times were ahead, was an exception. North Carolina's efforts at performance management and managing for results were factors in allowing the state to consider the strengths and weaknesses of some programs, and to conceive alternatives in the allocation of scarce resources.

Oregon provides another example of state management in a turbulent environment. In 1996 a citizen referendum (Ballot Measure 47) limited property tax revenue and pushed the state's budget into uncharted territory, quickly changing both revenues and expenditures. Oregon was an early leader in performance management and benchmarking, and the communication and planning links those activities provided to citizen advisory groups were valuable resources in rethinking priorities. Up-to-date information technology systems also facilitated information exchange and better decision making.

Federal agencies such as the Internal Revenue Service, the Patent and Trademark Office, and the Immigration and Naturalization Service are also examples of managing in very turbulent settings. The IRS, of course, encountered enormous and highly publicized difficulties with new information technology systems; these and other problems led the Congress to create an oversight board and to restructure leadership and top management positions in the organization. New leaders turned to redesigned human resources management systems as one part of the solution to rebuilding public and legislative confidence. The INS, battered by huge naturalization backlogs, the extreme shock of September 11 and its aftermath, proposals for dramatic reorganization, and an apparent inability to effectively address its problems, used new resources to beef up human resources; but it remains high on the list of very troubled organizations The Patent and Trademark Office was hampered in its ability to become a performance-based organization by difficult relations with its unions.

Good management is critical in these settings, and obviously some management resources must be expended on the crisis management or fire fighting that turbulence demands. Good management is also fundamental to the ability of new leadership to turn such a situation around. Effective change requires the institutional ability to support it; management can provide critical institutional capability in turbulence. In other words, management continues to matter, but it matters substantially more in terms of providing stability and direction to an organization under assault. Linking to substantive performance improvement is a longer-term objective.

When Does Management Matter Most?

Our results suggest that there are four circumstances in which management is likely to make the greatest difference: (1) where the government or agency has clear purpose and mission; (2) when the government or agency has flexibility to pursue that purpose; (3) where predictable action is valued for linking to results and performance; and(4) where new leadership requires institutional strength and support for effective change. These hypotheses are driven by our findings and represent fertile ground for future analysis.

Clear Purpose and Mission. The importance of clear mission emerged most specifically from our study of local governments and federal agencies but for different reasons in each setting. Achieving clarity of purpose and producing results around that purpose may be easier for local governments, whose services are evident to citizens on a daily and immediate basis. Citizens and elected officials know directly when fire and ambulance responses are too slow, when potholes are not filled, and when garbage is not collected. Furthermore, some forms of local government—notably council-manager governments—have an institutional capacity for clarity that does not exist in governments where power is more fragmented and diffuse. Still, the ability to link purpose to results is key. New York City's crime reduction and police performance tracking programs, for example, attracted international attention but were perhaps most notable for their simple objectives and their clarity. Limiting vandalism had an immediate impact: there were fewer broken windows, less graffiti, and, as a result, a greater feeling of security. The ability to track daily precinct performance against targets and objectives allowed the Police Department, elected officials, and citizens to chart continuing progress very closely; progress was defined in terms that everyone could understand.

At the federal level, where agency missions are often more a morass than a model of clarity, the Social Security Administration not only has a straightforward mission, but it has benefited from the spin-off from Health and Human Services in the mid-1990s. Independent agency status has allowed the SSA to limit its scope and mission. The National Weather Service has a clear mission largely because there is no great national debate about what the agency is supposed to do—we want it to predict the weather accurately and give sufficient lead times to promote public safety. Other efforts to introduce greater clarity at the federal level include the restructuring of the IRS—which still battles the incongruity of its two primary purposes: to collect taxes and to achieve high levels of citizen satisfaction in the process—and the designation of the Office of Student Financial Assistance and the Patent and Trademark Office as essentially single-purpose, performance-based organizations. At the other end of the spectrum, consider the Forest Service, which balances tree protection and timber harvesting. Under the Bush administration, sometimes with great difficulty: it is under pressure to make decisions that are more favorable to logging interests.

Flexibility and Discretion Coupled with Mission Clarity. Saying that having flexibility and discretion promotes effective management is not the same as the "let managers manage" message that was so integral a part of the Clinton administration's reinvention rhetoric (Osborne and Gaebler, 1992). Rather, it is a lesson that emphasizes supporting management activities and systems within a broad but clear framework of expectations and strategies.

The difference has to do with the pairing of authority to act with the clear accountability for the results that occur as the result of those actions. Stephen Goldsmith's competitive government initiatives did not tell the city agencies and unions in Indianapolis how to be competitive; however, they did clearly direct them toward competition.

Unfortunately, the combination of clear goals and missions coupled with the freedom to manage is rarely seen in the U.S. context. As Figure 7.1 indicates, examining goal clarity and managerial discretion presents the possibility that both could be present, that neither may be present, or that one or the other could be present.

Consider the two extremes. In a case where there is a low level of discretion but no clear agreement on goals, management becomes a rote process of following rules and procedures without any real appreciation for the context in which those rules and procedures exist. This is a traditional bureaucratic management paradigm, made perhaps more dysfunctional by the fact that there is constant confusion over goals and priorities. At the other end of the extreme is the case where there is general agreement on what the agency or government is intended to accomplish, coupled with the discretion to manage in a way that will enable that purpose to be achieved. This is the classic paradigm suggested by many "new public management" advocates (see Boston et al., 1996), who suggest that the coupling of "clarity of task and purpose" and managerial discretion provides the optimal scenario for successful results-based management. This is because managers have both the luxury of knowing what they are expected to accomplish and the ability to design management strategies to accomplish these objectives.

Government organizations in the United States do not tend to fall neatly on either of these extremes. Necessity has dictated that there is a substantial degree of discretion in government agencies simply because elected officials delegate many details of policy to these agencies. The prevailing orthodox view of public administration in the early part of the twentieth century suggested a separation between "policy" and "administration," reducing administration to purely a technical enterprise. The recognition of the important role that discretion played in the policy process led to the discrediting of the "politics-administration dichotomy" more than fifty years ago. On the other hand, this discretion is not total. Managers continually decry "red tape" and regulations that they believe prevent them from focusing on mission-critical work. The Clinton administration's National Performance Review, in calling for more managerial discretion, criticized a management environment where "process is our most important product."

Level of Discretion

	Low	High
Low	**1** Little clarity or discretion— traditional bureaucratic control coupled with mission confusion.	**2** Substantial managerial flexibility but little agreement on goals. High potential for misplaced discretion since goals are subject to misinterpretation and confusion.
High	**3** Clear missions but limited ability for agencies or governments to act creatively or flexibly to design management strategies that will maximize the probability of success.	**4** Clear goals coupled with flexibility to achieve goals. High probability of success using new public management paradigm.

Level of Clarity (left axis label)

Figure 7.1. Clarity/discretion matrix

Figure 7.1 presents a matrix where agencies exist according to the presence of clarity, on the one hand, and discretion to act, on the other. We would suggest that there are substantial differences between government organizations, depending on where they fall in this matrix (note that neither clarity or discretion are dichotomous; rather they exist on a continuum). If we consider each of these four cells in turn, we can use our findings to illustrate what are likely to be the opportunities and challenges for management in each case.

Cell 1: Limited Clarity, Limited Discretion. First consider cell 1, where there is little clarity and little discretion. This is the traditional bureaucratic paradigm, where organizations are prevented by rules and procedures from exercising discretion. Coupled with this, however, is very limited capacity to understand the overall goals of the organization. This could be either because there is no consistent set of directions for the organization or because there is such conflict between different missions as to give employees no clear indication of a framework in which to act. The likelihood of systemic success in this environment is very low. For example, part of the inherent problem of the Immigration and Naturalization Service, as noted, is that it is constantly buffeted between its "enforcement" and "service" missions. INS employees are also hampered by an inability to direct resources to where they are most needed and are often not permitted to take actions in individual circumstances that would results in better achievement of any of the agency's competing missions.

Cell 2: Limited Clarity, Substantial Discretion. Most organizations do not exist in an environment where both clarity and discretion are severely limited. Most exist in a managerial environment where they have some discretion (that is, where there is policymaking delegation but still a substantial degree of process control), or some clarity but very limited discretion. It seems reasonable to conclude that in the United States, government organizations tend to fall most neatly into cells 2 and 3. In cell 2, where there is little goal clarity, even an agency or government where there is discretion may be "flying blind"; that is, it may not matter very much how much discretion an organization has if it does not know what it is intending to accomplish.

Consider a case of a law enforcement agency where so-called street-level bureaucrats have substantial autonomy in terms of determining how aggressively to pursue suspected lawbreakers. If this discretion is exercised without regard for its consistency with overall policy goals (with a desire to reduce particular types of crime, for example) it will result, at best, in inconsistent and uncoordinated policy. The Forest Service may be the best federal example of this phenomenon. Our evaluation of the Forest Service indicated substantial autonomy for managers at the level of an individual national forest but very limited capacity for central management in Washington to pursue a national strategy. This was in part because of problems with information sharing between headquarters and the field, and in part because of the Forest Service's multiple priorities. This situation may result in very good results in individual cases, but these results are highly dependent on the actions of individual managers and are not easily or consistently sustainable across the entire organization.

The experience of the states with centralization and decentralization of human resource management activities is another example. Strongly decentralized systems provided very substantial discretion but limited clarity in terms of what was being achieved—or attempted—government-wide. The move back toward strategic balancing remedies that problem.

Cell 3: Substantial Clarity, Limited Discretion. On the other hand, providing clear goals without the authority to pursue management strategies that maximize the potential to achieve those goals is a recipe for achieving suboptimal results. It is this precise situation that has led to the movement in many countries toward a new public management framework that emphasizes freedom to pursue management strategies unencumbered by traditional bureaucratic rules. This paradigm was embodied in both the Clinton administration's "reinventing government" initiative and in the Bush administration's "Freedom to Manage" legislation. Examples abound of agencies that are prevented by bureaucratic rules from taking actions that would contribute to mission success. The Postal Service, as one case, is inhibited in its drive to maintain financial self-sufficiency by a number of factors, including lack of control of rate-setting, inability to limit service to high-cost areas, and inability to relocate personnel because of union agreements. Cities and states that "reinvented" their management systems without fundamental reform of legislative bases were similarly inhibited.

Cell 4: Substantial Clarity, Substantial Discretion. There are probably fewer government organizations in cell 4 than in any of the other three. At the extreme end of this continuum, one would find a fully mature government or agency with a clear understanding of what it is to accomplish, strong and effective leadership, and the ability to use all the tools necessary to accomplish its mission. It would also be essential for such an ideal example to have accountability for results in order to ensure that discretion was used appropriately. We found organizations and governments that are moving in the direction of cell 4, even if most are not there yet. The National Weather Service has a clear mission and is attempting to increase discretion; the Federal Aviation Administration has been freed from many personnel and other constraints but still (particularly since September 11) suffers from clear mission conflict. Phoenix prizes clarity and flexibility and consciously pursues both, as do Virginia and Washington.

Human resources and information technology systems were the two management systems that were most often the target of reforms intended to provide more flexibility for managers. Decentralization reforms in human resources management exemplify the need to provide some framework and basic information and coordination system to managers and others while still allowing for discretion. In the initial moves toward strongly decentralized systems, agencies and managers were given broad discretion in recruiting, testing, hiring, and other core human resource management activities. Central agencies, often including the governor's office and the budget office, were not able to gather necessary information about the state of the workforce, however, nor were they able to strategically identify problems or to plan ahead. Newly "rebalanced" systems provide broad principles and guidelines from the center and flexibility within that framework.

Information technology management reflects the same principles. At all of the levels of government we studied, the initial IT strategy was decentralized within governments and within agencies. In combination with complex procurement laws and regulations, this led to a series of outdated systems that did not talk to one another and to vastly different capabilities across management systems. The obvious impact was to hinder decision making and to limit the usefulness of whatever information was gathered. Furthermore, the simple ability of governments to meet the challenges many believed would be imposed by Y2K was very much in doubt. The response—again widespread— was to create a central locus for coordination, generally in the form of a chief information officer, thereby providing broad direction but also the continuing opportunity for flexible tailoring within the framework.

Predictable Action for Linking Management to Results. Increasingly, governments are turning to results-based systems to track performance against goals and objectives. Most of the states, for example, now have managing for results legislation on the books. Melkers and Willoughby (1998) observe that forty-seven of the fifty states have some kind of legislative or administrative requirement; fully two-thirds of these are legislative mandates. The federal government has the Government Performance and Results Act. Passing legislation is only one—and perhaps the least significant— part of the process, however, because the reality is in implementation. For the desired results to be attained, the government or agency must have the ability to align resources with priorities, to manage to priorities, and to evaluate progress. That capacity logically relies on strong management systems and consistent managerial ability.

The intervening role that management capacity plays in linking activities and programs to performance is evident in several ways. First, the measurement process itself—an endemic problem for public organizations—is heavily dependent on consistent learning. Governments' and agencies' ability to move from simple measures of output to more sophisticated outcome measures is iterative. No government or agency included in the GPP/FPP analysis believed that they had gotten the measures right the first or the second time, but they consistently described the learning curve as fundamental to a good system.

Second, while governments and agencies will never operate in a totally predictable environment, the ability to match resource expenditures to objectives and promised targets is central to effective performance management. Measurement systems can provide information about good performance; they can also describe where and when the train went off the track. They cannot keep the train on the track. Only leaders and good managers can do that.

Finally, good management systems can provide leaders, elected officials, and citizens with information about why public programs perform—or do not perform—well. Explanations of results need to include those internal to the organization. The expertise and institutional knowledge necessary for this dimension reside with top management and the systems they administer. One city noted that, while one objective of their managing for results (MFR) system was to continue to improve measurement, an equally important goal was to continue to develop "management expertise in understanding, utilizing, and analyzing the information that [MFR reports] provide."

Where New Leadership Requires Support. Most often in the literature, leaders are characterized as free floating; that is, the leaders are described as "energizing," "revitalizing," or "reconstructing" the organization (Bass, 1985). Some of these descriptions sound as if leadership actions are independent and unilateral. That, of course, is not the case, particularly in public organizations. As the next section of this chapter describes in more detail, the leaders identified in the GPP and the FPP are "grounded" leaders. They bring strengths and vision to the organization but also draw on—or create—more purely organizational strengths to achieve their objectives (Ulrich, Zenger, and Smallwood, 1999; Ingraham, 2001).

An important part of such organizational strength is the management capacity created by effective and integrated systems. That capacity creates the ability, as one leader put it, "to turn left when I ask the organization to turn left." This ability is particularly important when the organization in undergoing change. Early successes in change efforts are important; early failures poison the effort for the longer term. Furthermore, unrealistic expectations—particularly those related to the timing of reform impacts—set the agency or government up for failure. Effective leaders therefore identify the systems and the actors they will need for success early on and use them or build them as quickly as possible.

The synergy we found between strong leadership and strong management cannot be overemphasized. It appears that leaders can indeed provide energy and vision, but support in the form of a strong management team is required to move the organization constructively forward. This idea, which is elaborated below, also suggests that future analyses of government management systems would benefit from including new criteria that more directly capture the effects we have begun to identify.

Effective Leadership Is Vital

The GPP and FPP did not set out to study or analyze leadership per se. Instead, we focused on the ability of governments and agencies to manage toward results, to build effective management systems, and to align and integrate them in productive ways. Yet in every case where we found strength in these areas, we also found a strong leader or leadership team. Conversely, those governments and agencies that struggled with management and performance were notable for the absence of leadership and direction. This section describes preliminary hypotheses about leadership that appear stable in light of our findings and that we believe are likely to be validated in future work.

We identified leaders and leadership teams following two general methodologies. First, as Meier and Gill (2000) note, it is high-performing governments and organizations that draw the most lesson-learning attention. As in Lake Wobegon, being average is not very interesting, and most governments or agencies that wish to improve do not seek out failed organizations as models. Therefore, we began by examining the differences between high-performing governments and agencies and those that did not do so well. We then essentially applied backward mapping techniques to observe commonalities in high performers (Bardach, 2000). Leadership quickly became an obvious variable. It is reasonable to assume that good leadership was significant because it is central to the creation, maintenance, and refreshing of a long-term vision for the government or agency; because it is key to integrating management systems and activities with strategic priorities; and because strong leaders clearly link results to accountability. The second methodology was to examine specific examples of demonstrated leadership in more depth, exploring strategies and priorities, particularly as they related to communication and integration of activities across government.

Vision

Earlier, we discussed the need for clarity in mission and purpose in public organizations. Leaders serve two very important roles in this regard: they set or limit mission boundaries, and they enforce the integrity of those boundaries to the greatest extent possible. The focus this provides to organizational activities is intuitively central to the pursuit of better performance. Furthermore, the ability to state and defend limited purpose and clear priorities—as simple as it may sound—is hard to come by in public organizations. Strong leaders were successful in this regard across the board in the governments and agencies we studied.

In the federal government, for example, Dr. Kenneth Kizer drove the vision of a restructured healthcare delivery system for veterans throughout the decentralized Veterans' Health Administration. He successfully improved service at lower cost but found it necessary to defend the new structure every step of the way. Similarly, James Lee Witt took a disorganized and sluggish Federal Emergency Management Agency, gave it more specific objectives and tighter performance guidelines, successfully defended the need for the changes, and rejuvenated the organization. Admiral James Loy became the first Coast Guard commandant in recent memory to attempt to get the Congress and the administration to confront the mismatch between creeping mission requirements and resources.

In Washington, Governor Gary Locke described decentralized state government as too big and slow to respond to citizens, proclaimed better and more understandable technology to be a big part of the solution, and brought the state to the forefront of governments' ability to speed and simplify service delivery. Governor John Kitzhaber led the way to unprecedented funding agreements with the federal government as a way of taking Oregon to more solid (if still troubled) budgetary ground. The late Governor Mel Carnahan concluded that Missouri's famous reputation as the "show me" state should be, not just rhetoric, but the guideline for how governments related to their citizens. Performance reports for major state agencies are now posted and updated monthly on the state's "Show Me" Web site.

City governments also demonstrate the positive effects of strong leadership. As part of a joint political-professional team, the city manager of Phoenix, Frank Fairbanks, has led the city to national and international recognition as a model of open government and excellent management. Minneapolis, a city with a very diffuse power base in its city government, benefited from the leadership skills of its former mayor, Sharon Sayles Belton, in addressing strategic planning and citizen involvement needs.

Integration

In the GPP/FPP model and throughout the analysis, we have emphasized that integration among management systems was likely to contribute to greater management capacity and higher potential for performance. The governments and agencies we examined agreed that this was true. The most important lesson here, however, is that integration is neither an obvious

choice for governments nor an easy process. The tendency to treat management systems as "stovepipes" is strong, particularly because employees are
often very specialized: they know a lot about their specific area of responsibility but often are not focused on the big picture. In fact, we found that
integration occurred only when a strong leader or leadership team made it a
priority.

We also found, however, that even in the presence of strong leadership,
building an integrated performance-based government is a progressive,
building-block process. Leaders and leadership teams identified and pursued different strategies for performance, but all were cumulative, creating
capacity in one area and then building on it for greater strength and capacity
elsewhere. The state of Virginia is a leading example. A key component of
Virginia's leadership cadre is a polished and talented set of career managers
who worked for some time to establish the budgetary and financial management systems in Virginia as models for performance and drivers of change.
Commissioner of Finance Ron Tillett was in place through two gubernatorial administrations and served as a consistent voice for performance and
integration. Integration occurred because as the budget system became
more sophisticated, other systems necessarily were reformed and revised to
be compatible. Overall, Virginia provides many of the critical components
and links to successful integration: strategic direction, staff expertise and
commitment, information technology support, and legislative reform to
support the goals and practices of government-wide system integration (for
example, civil service reform in 1999).

The Washington model is somewhat different but works from essentially
the same recipe. Governor Locke spearheaded the effort to end Washington's
"decentralization sprawl" and to build statewide support for performance
initiatives. The governor's "Washington State Priorities" provide the overarching framework for agency planning; a 1997 Executive Order directs
agencies to develop and implement programs to improve service delivery; a
balanced scorecard approach addresses cross-agency and system performance management; and performance measurement results are included in
the state budget. Information technology architecture that is standardized
across agencies provides another dimension of integration.

Phoenix provides an excellent example at the city level, as does the Coast
Guard for the federal government. Both work from the foundation of a very
strong set of core values. Leaders in both settings have successfully created a
more integrated set of systems by emphasizing an overall business strategy
for the organization and by aligning systems to the greatest extent possible

within the framework of the strategic objectives. There is a clear commitment to employee involvement in both planning and evaluation.

At the federal level, Admiral Loy and his immediate predecessors at the Coast Guard, bolstered by an extraordinary cadre of subordinate managers and executives, have fostered a culture where decisions made in the context of all management areas are considered in light of their contribution to agency results. The National Weather Service, with its commitment to the goal of becoming a "no surprise" service, is another example. When NWS completed its technology modernization effort recently after several false starts, it was largely because Director Jack Kelly encouraged attention to the mission implications of technology.

The idea that strong leaders are attentive to integration across management systems comports well with the definitions of leadership and performance outlined by Ulrich, Zenger, and Smallwood (1999), who argue that high performance is attributable to the synergy between organizational capital and human capital. The grounded leaders the GPP and the FPP found in public organizations—like Admiral Loy, Director Kelly, Doctor Kizer, City Manager Fairbanks, Commissioner Tillett, and Governor Locke—used their leadership and positional status as integrating devices to focus existing organizational strengths and to create new ones. Among these leaders and the others we identified, we found several common leadership practices:

- Early and specific identification of leadership base and strength
- Clear statement and frequent reinforcing of strategic values, vision, and priorities
- Capacity building around priorities
- Progressive building of integrating mechanisms and communications
- Strong focus on implementation.

Linking Results and Accountability

Mayors are obvious examples of a direct link between leadership, government performance, and accountability. As noted earlier, service delivery and civic access are more simply assessed and described in local governments. Mayors are in parades, on the streets, and in neighborhood meetings and are frequent subjects of media coverage. They are readily identified with city government. Even for mayors, however—and most certainly for leaders at other levels of government—linking promised or desired action to results that citizens can observe and understand is tough.

Strong leaders are likely to be important to capacity and performance because they address and clarify the performance-accountability link; they set the boundaries for expected and acceptable performance and enforce both the boundaries and performance standards. Leaders accept the responsibility for results-based government when the results are good but also when they are not so good. This "for better or for worse" linkage is fundamental to a performance and accountability structure that citizens trust. As noted in Chapter 6, for example, the Veterans Health Administration held Veterans Integrated Service Network directors accountable through individual contracts that prominently featured patient health goals. Indianapolis and New York City provide examples at the local level, as do Missouri and Utah at the state level.

If bad news is a catastrophe and not a basis for learning and adjustment, however, managing for results is a farce. One city in the GPP analysis provided a classic example. That city observed that talking about performance in good economic times was not necessary because nobody cared, and in bad times it was only a blaming exercise. This is one reason that examples such as Phoenix are so important to public organizations. The mantra in Phoenix—"There is always something we can do better"—combined with that city's openness and candor about performance, illustrates well the positive linking between results and accountability that we found in strongly led governments and agencies.

Criteria-based Assessment Facilitates Learning

Criteria-based assessment is a common tool in organizational analysis. The Baldrige criteria and the criteria developed by the European Foundation for Quality Management are widely known and used examples. The GPP/FPP criteria, however, are unusual in three ways. First, they were developed specifically for, and to some extent by, public organizations. Second, they focus on all of the critical internal systems common to public organizations —the emphasis on human resources management, information management, and capital and infrastructure management is rare—and on the qualities that "publicness" brings to those systems. Finally, because the criteria are transparent, they are well known to participating governments throughout the analysis. They were reexamined after every year's cycle in learning conferences and other meetings between participants and GPP/FPP staff.

This approach facilitates learning across the governments analyzed because it provides common points of reference but also supports comparative lesson drawing. As a result, comparisons emerge in relation to structure (and balance within different structures), political and economic environments, leadership strategies, and, of course, across management systems. Of most significance, however, the foundation provided by the application of common criteria allowed distinctions between high-capacity and lower-capacity governments to be drawn. The widespread consensus about the content of the criteria created a much better ability to discuss the relative abilities of governments and their managers objectively, and each year saw greater consensus than the year before, largely as a result of the extensive consultation.

The human resources management systems we studied, for example, reflected some commonalities, as would be anticipated. But particularly in the two-year comparisons of the states, there were also remarkable differences. Movement along the centralization/decentralization continuum, diffusion of new practices and policies, and even debate about the utility of civil service systems in modern organizations contributed to widely disparate patterns across the fifty states. In some cases (the movement from decentralized human resources functions to more strategically balanced systems, for example), the different patterns reflected substantive political and policy differences. In others, economic variations provided a more direct explanation.

There are a number of interrelated explanations for the variations. Generally, the variations and comparisons can be grouped into the following categories, which closely parallel the model presented in Chapter 3: the nature of the systems themselves (the extent to which they were simplified and flexible or more traditional and narrow); the setting of the management systems (the environment of the government); the structure of the government and of the management systems within it (centralized or decentralized, for example); and the strategy or strategies pursued by the government in efforts to attain better capacity. A fifth component, which we have referred to as integration, may also be defined as synergy among the systems that allows individual system capacity to feed into a broader potential for performance (Ingraham, and Kneedler, 2000b). We have already discussed three of these—systems, synergy, and strategy—and results have been reviewed in Chapters 5 and 6. The grades assigned to the various systems do demonstrate variation and different capabilities to address the capacity for performance, and analyses based on them demonstrate the utility of the criteria-based approach for differentiating levels of capacity.* Some of the broader lessons, however, are equally compelling. We will focus our discussion on setting and structure.

Setting

In discussing the setting of management, for example, we did not anticipate that there would be regional or political differences in capacity creation. Rather, we argued that the analysis would proceed from the assumption that capacity could occur anywhere, in any setting, and would depend largely on the extent to which resources and talents that were present were used carefully and strategically. Although we were correct in assuming that regional or political factors would not stand out as major contributors to variation, we did find that setting made a difference.†

The presence of highly charged or politicized labor-management relationships (as in the Patent and Trademark Office or the Postal Service at the federal level, and the state of New York and the city of Buffalo, for example) had a major impact on how some of the entities we analyzed were able to think about and organize their management systems. Similarly, the high-tech environment in which the state of Washington conducts its business has had a clear impact on how that state views technology as a successful management tool. Previous public policy decisions created a constrained budgetary setting for states such as California and Oregon and cities such as Seattle; many other states encountered similar shortfalls in 2001 and 2002. Capacity in many of the management systems, therefore—but particularly in financial management—was heavily influenced by economic realities. Virtually all of the states and cities were benefiting from a booming economy over the first three years of the study. This undoubtedly influenced the relatively high grades in financial management, since many of the undesirable practices (such as borrowing from pension funds or failing to support rainy-day funds, for example) were less likely to occur. Setting and environment influenced choices about management systems both directly—by lim-

*GPP results are posted at the project Web site at www.maxwell.syr.edu/gpp; Joyce, 2001; Joyce and Tompkins, 2002; Ingraham and Moynihan, 2000; Selden, Jacobsen, and Ingraham, 1999; Jacobson, Rubin, and Selden, 2000; Hou, Duncombe, Ammar, and Wright, 2000; *Governing*, February 2001, February 2000, and February 1999; *Government Executive*, April 2001, March 2000, February 1999.
†For a discussion of the role of setting in the context of public schools, see Broderick, Jacob, and Bryk, 2000.

iting resource availability—and indirectly—by creating an environment for decisions and choice based on predominating values or priorities.

Structure

Structure also proved to be more complex than initial assumptions suggested. Much of the management reform literature argues that standardized, centralized structures are not conducive to capacity and performance and that more flexible organizations and systems are preferable (see Osborne and Gaebler, 1992; Barzelay and Armajani, 1991). The expectation was that organizations seeking to streamline and improve management systems would move toward a more decentralized and streamlined model; however, the GPP analysis leads to a much more nuanced conclusion.

Location or region did play some role here. The eastern industrial states tended to have more rigid, centralized structures than did other regions of the country, for example. Management systems reflected this hierarchy and centralization. Even governments that otherwise qualify as strongly centralized, however, have been modified somewhat by various reform and simplification measures. Other governments, such as Pennsylvania, argued that its centralized human resource management system was crucial to effective government.

Decentralization strategies appeared to be increasingly popular when the first GPP state survey was conducted in 1998. The 2000 survey revealed a different pattern: a move back toward the center and an effort to structurally balance centralizing and decentralizing forces, so that strategy and general direction setting remains—or becomes—a central function but problem definition and implementation are decentralized. In the case of information technology, the move toward chief information officers is strongly centralizing, but that role is much stronger in the oversight of effective implementation than it is in the case of system or architecture design. In addition, the Y2K crisis encouraged centralization, at least until it was clear that potential problems with Y2K compliance had been resolved. Furthermore, entities such as the National Weather Service, Internal Revenue Service, or the Health Care Financing Administration at the federal level that had a history of failed IT systems tended to centralize in order to coordinate organizational learning and prevent a repeat of previous failures.

The pattern of balancing centralization and decentralization is also evident in the two states that represent the decentralized end of the spectrum, Texas and Georgia. Texas is broadly decentralized. Georgia effectively decentralized its human resources system by abolishing the merit system on the books in 1996. Both states are recognizing the need for some centralization in terms of information and general strategy, however. Texas worries that it does not have enough information about what is happening at the agency level to make valid decisions about statewide needs and demands. General comparability in areas such as performance appraisal and reward are also a concern. Georgia is in the process of designing and implementing central guidance to agencies in the state government as they struggle to achieve the fundamental purpose of a statewide human resources system without legislation that provides clear general direction. In both cases, the benefits of decentralization are being balanced with the need for the central information and data critical to effective decision making and guidance.

The Road to Change is Long and Painful but Taken Nonetheless

The GPP and the FPP have demonstrated that the appetite and capacity for learning and change in public organizations is substantial. Despite this fact, change in the public sector is often a bumpy process with mixed results. The variations discussed above account for only some of the differences in change experiences. Differences—and even success or failure—are often masked by the tendency to evaluate public change processes after too short a time or to interpret them as discrete events. Ineffective change in public organizations is most often attributed to the volume and frequency of change efforts, to lack of agreement on change strategy, or to simple bureaucratic recalcitrance (Pressman and Wildavsky, 1984; Light, 1997; Thompson, 2000). Similarly, opportunities for organizational learning are perceived to be limited and frequently not utilized (J. Wilson, 1989).

The GPP/FPP findings, however, describe a different reality. To be sure, we found governments and agencies that were completely satisfied with the status quo. We found many more, however, with high interest in learning from others and from the comparisons emerging from the analyses. Moreover, we found that the progressive building-block approach described in previous chapters in terms of managing for results and capacity building was also an apt description of the general strategy by which governments and agencies pursued change. This interpretation is not intended to overlook failure or to sugarcoat resistance to change. That both occur in public as well as private organizations is well recognized. Rather, it is to note that learning is a lumpy process, to which less than full success and even failure contributes. Several of the management systems analyzed demonstrate these points.

Managing for Results

There is a long history of efforts to introduce more of a performance orientation to government, seen in reforms such as Planning, Programming, and Budgeting Systems (PPBS), Zero Based Budgeting (ZBB), Management by Objectives (MBO), and others. In many respects, the "tides of reform" description seems appropriate to change efforts directed at performance management (Light, 1997). At the same time, however, the GPP/FPP studies point to a long-term learning process at all levels of government in which some elements of previous reforms are retained for purposes of future reform. PPBS may well have been judged a short-term failure by some standards, but the federal agencies we studied had learned important lessons from it, which are reflected in their approach to performance management today—meeting the requirements of the Government Performance and Results Act, for example. Likewise, state and local governments are in a much better position to implement the latest round of performance management reforms because they developed capacity from attempts to implement past reforms that were likely decried as failures at the time. Indeed, many of the problems that exist today appear more attributable to conflicting legislative objectives and oversight measures than to internal management problems.

Human Resources Management

Human resources management systems and efforts to change them have many of the same attributes as managing for results systems. For many governments and all federal agencies, the starting point for change was a crusty old civil service system. Early efforts at change did not generally address the core structure; instead, they tinkered at the fringes (Ingraham, 1995). Government managers—if not always other reformers (NPR, 1997)— quickly learned that did not work. Subsequent reforms in the states strongly advocated movement away from a rigid central model to decentralized authority and discretion. In many cases, these reforms too were judged ineffective (Ingraham and Selden, 2001). Current efforts strive to achieve a strategic balance that allows for flexibility and discretion but within a clear framework of core principles and guidelines.

It is important to note here that the federal system continues to operate with an exception-based model rather than with a fundamentally reformed model. For many federal agencies—including most of those included in the analysis—the federal civil service system and code continues to be the structural framework for human resources systems. In the case of federal agencies, the exceptions (FAA, IRS) provide the learning examples.

Information Management Systems

Systems to manage technology present a slightly different but important case. The Y2K scare raised serious questions about the ability of governments and agencies to meet daily service-delivery demands. Many governments agreed that their IT capacity would, at best, be challenged. Solving the technology problem quickly and with limited financial resources required a strong problem-solving ability. It also relied on the set of lessons learned from previous IT design, purchase, installation, and use changes. Unlike the case of human resources or managing for results, the lessons and best practices had to be applied quickly, all at once, and to bypass more step-by-step capacity-building processes. In many settings, the new presence of a chief information officer assisted in the coordination and problem-solving activities.

In all cases, past experiences provided learning opportunities and potential stepping-stones to the new capacity required. The second survey of the states in 2000 reflects the ability of governments to apply lessons learned to critical change activities: the average IT grade rose by a full grade from the 1998 level. Obviously of more significance, the Y2K "crisis" passed by very quietly. The earlier discussion of building blocks for capacity over a period of time suggests that public organization's time frame for change is necessarily long, and in many cases that is true. The Y2K lesson demonstrates that, even though lesson learning in public organizations can be long term, this does not preclude rapid application and successful short-term results when conditions demand. There is another set of lessons related to changing management systems that is equally important and very commonly overlooked. That is the role played by management systems and reforms to them as policy tools.

Management Systems Are Policy Levers for Improvement

Throughout the GPP, the FPP, and this book, we have argued that if public sector performance is to be fully understood, it is necessary to more carefully specify the "middle of the performance equation"; that is, the capacity of the organization to translate resources into results. We have also argued that the management systems common to government organizations are a crucial component of that capacity. If the quality and ability of those systems is improved, we said, so is the potential capacity of the organization to meet performance objectives effectively. Thus, if we think in terms of the levers available to public leaders and elected officials for whom better performance is a policy goal, management systems should be an obvious target. It is clear that some components of the policy process are not malleable; the model we have relied on throughout the studies clarifies that point. For public organizations, externally controlled financial resources and political support are variables that provide ample evidence of volatility and lack of manipulability. Moreover, it is evident from our analysis and others that those characteristics of management systems that are most conducive to improved performance are also the ones least likely to be supported when the political environment is unfriendly or volatile—flexibility and discretion are clear examples.

Nonetheless, we have found that leaders and managers at every level of government understand that, if the goal is better performance, clear purpose and good assessment skills are not sufficient drivers of performance. Public organizations must also have the capacity to perform. Capacity can be changed by changing or reforming financial management and information technology management (or human resources or capital management systems), as well as by creating the integration among management systems that a good managing for results system supports. Earlier analyses have demonstrated that there is no shortage of legislative and other efforts to alter management systems (Light, 1997). The problem is that relatively few of them are intended to create capacity; too many are directed at control or fall into the "flavor of the month" category of reform.

In the high-performance governments and agencies we studied, we found this not to be the case. Rather—as in the cases of the Coast Guard, the Social Security Administration, and the National Weather Service; the states of Washington, Utah, and Virginia; and cities such as Phoenix, Indianapolis, Milwaukee, and Austin—the goal was to enhance transparency about the systems and integration among them. Leaders understood that it was their responsibility to set parameters and provide support. In these settings, the utility of effective management systems was clear, and the effort to create formal policy foundations to support them was a significant part of a grounded leadership strategy. There was also frequent recognition that policy change in one management system would necessarily drive more informal changes in others.

In less favorable circumstances, the need to use whatever resources were available in the best possible way was equally clear. Policy leaders and GPP/ FPP staff were inundated with requests for information about specific content of legislation and other proposed or recent changes in high-performing governments and agencies. Even in the absence of specific empirical links between specific characteristics of management and improved performance, it is evident that governments understand the link; those that know how resources are used and for what purpose are in a stronger position than those governments that cannot make that connection.

The Grading Process Itself Stimulated Change

The grading process in the GPP/FPP was intended to be a learning exercise for entities studied and for the public; in particular, they were to provide the opportunities for governments and agencies to learn from one another. That definitely happened; in fact, in some instances the clamor for more information outpaced the ability of the GPP and the FPP to provide it. As the projects progressed, it became more and more evident that another purpose was being served: to provide a widely agreed upon definition of "good" management.

Both teachers and practitioners of the art and science of public management have argued that "management matters," but there was little consistent definition of what management is, what it was about management that mattered, and why. The criteria-based assessment of the projects provided widespread consensus about a working definition of good management as well as general guidelines about how it mattered. This consensus allowed commonsense agreement that, if these criteria broadly defined good management systems, it was worth working to achieve the systems and practices they described.

The appetite for learning was evident in both high- and low-capacity governments. The state of Virginia, a leader in both years of state analysis, actively pursued lessons from other states that they perceived to have better systems. In the area of human resource management systems, for example, this learning resulted in 1999 civil service reform legislation. The city of Phoenix, deluged with requests for information about its systems and success, posted its entire GPP survey on its Web site to meet the demand. The state of Alabama, whose new governor was frustrated by low grades in year one of the state survey, sent members of his management team to higher-capacity states and to the GPP staff to observe and learn. The governor of New Jersey requested that GPP lessons be translated to the management of smaller distressed cities. There were many international requests related to the conceptual model and lessons learned. These are but a few examples of the widespread interest in learning.

The learning activities and communication this spawned have been described elsewhere in this chapter and book. The broad point here is that because the GPP/FPP activities were not punitive exercises, because the criteria represent broad practical and academic consensus, and because the process is transparent, the grades and the publicity surrounding them became significant motivators for change. In the context of a constructive dialogue about public management capacity and performance, the governments involved in this study and many others seized upon the opportunity to evaluate existing systems and to initiate change. Furthermore, the broad representativeness of the governments and agencies studied ensured that there were lessons, models, and potential solutions to many problems from other public organizations. In the final analysis, five words sum it up: *governments care about effective management.* That is the major lesson of both the GPP and the FPP. Next steps in assisting governments, agencies, and their managers—as well as those who study them—in linking this concern to better performance are outlined in the final chapter.

8 | Next Steps

The Government Performance Project (GPP) and Federal Performance Project (FPP) have, as described in the preceding chapters, been successful in highlighting effective management practices across three levels of U.S. government. The continuing challenge for analysts interested in understanding what contributes to effective public management is to build on these lessons. In this final chapter, we summarize the contributions of the projects and provide a proposed "road map" to follow in the continuing search for improved management practice and better government.

What Progress Did the GPP and FPP Make?

Together, the GPP and FPP made a number of contributions to the concrete analysis and measurement of management and to supporting improvements in management. These include conceptual progress, methodological contributions, practical contributions, and links to other research and to other capacity-building activities.

Conceptual Progress

At its outset, the project faced a daunting task: to measure a concept and activity (effective management) about whose *definition* there was less-than-uniform agreement in the literature and among experts. One of the key contributions of the projects, therefore, has been to make progress on developing consensus about what constitutes effective management practice. To be sure, there was more agreement in some issue areas than others. But the process of measuring, getting feedback, and remeasuring has resulted in substantial discussion and greater consensus over time.

The projects have made particular progress in two areas. First, they have focused on understanding the role that managing for results plays in leveraging broader management effectiveness. Second, they highlighted the importance of integration across management systems. In the first case, the time frame of the project coincided with a return to prominence of results-based management. Governments throughout the world are focusing more resolutely on results and attempting to determine how they can identify strategic objectives and effectively measure progress against them.

In addition, the projects have explicitly attempted to look at management systems, not as ends in themselves, but as parts of a broader integrated management framework. Large bureaucracies are by nature specialized, but this specialization carries a cost. Narrow specialization inhibits understanding of how the different pieces of the organization fit together to serve a broad purpose. A state personnel director, for example, may be concerned with the nuts and bolts of personnel policy but may have difficulty focusing on government-wide workforce planning. A chief information officer may know a great deal about IT architecture but may not be focused on getting information to people when they need it—or to the right people in a format they can use.

Methodological Contributions

Because the projects represent the largest and most systematic effort to measure the quality of management using rigorous and consistent techniques, the potential for methodological progress was great. Here, the GPP/FPP contribution has been to demonstrate not only that management can be studied and described in methodologically robust ways but also that multiple sources of data and multiple methods can be brought together to evaluate and draw lessons from governments and government agencies.

What the projects did *not* do is equally important. Early on, many argued that a "ranking governments" exercise—listing the states from one to fifty, for example—would be desirable. The projects chose not to do so. Such measurement systems are necessarily vastly oversimplified. The complex realities of governments and their managerial environments do not fairly translate into minute differences between number one and number two—or numbers forty-nine and fifty. Creating a fair assessment process that did no harm to the governments and agencies studied was a consistent priority for the projects. Avoiding ranking, the grading methodology chosen instead was an effort to sort governments and agencies into categories or grades based on management capacity. Just as in classroom grading, the differences between grade levels were clear and significant; differences within each grade level were not emphasized.

In addition, the use of multiple data sources, analytic techniques, and raters decreased the chances of getting the grades and the conclusions wrong. Detailed surveys of central governments and agencies enabled those that were being evaluated to tell their own stories. The questions in the survey were extensively field-tested and were subject to comment and revision after each year. Information from the surveys was analyzed rigorously and from many perspectives. When necessary, additional information was gathered to supplement and clarify that in the survey. Interviews by journalists of internal staff and external stakeholders provided additional information to assist in verifying information collected from the government or agency. Reviews of relevant documents were also an important source of information. Often these documents themselves provided an external perspective on agency or government management. This was true, for example, of audits of Comprehensive Annual Financial Reports at the state and local level, or GAO reports at the federal level. The use of qualitative and quantitative approaches to analyzing data and establishing ratings of state and local governments made it much less likely that errors in interpretation would be made or that we would be inconsistent in our application of the criteria. The use of the managers' survey at the federal level made it less likely that inflated conclusions about agencies would emerge.

This self-conscious reliance on multiple methods is unusual, but its strength provides a significant research lesson when the objective is the analysis of complex organizations. The diversity of methods employed in the GPP and the FPP will not always be available, of course. For example, the projects relied on a partnership of journalists and academics—unusual for many reasons. For the purposes of these projects, however, there were benefits. Good journalists are simply better at interviewing than good academics. Good academics are simply better at attending to methodological rigor than good journalists. The result for the GPP and the FPP was clearly a situation in which the whole was greater than the sum of its parts. For other analysts, the benefit of multiple perspectives is the lesson to be learned.

Practical Contributions

As well as improving the understanding of management and permitting more methodologically valid assessments of management, the projects were intended to make a practical difference. They were, we believe, successful on this score in three ways. First, the level of media discourse in the broader press (beyond *Governing* and *Government Executive* magazines) concerning management issues was extraordinary, exceeding expectations. Major newspapers, smaller dailies, editorial page writers, TV news reporters, and even talk show hosts reported on the grades and their implications for the state, city, or agency closest to home. The stories that appeared were largely not "gotcha" stories, nor were they stories that focused on who might gain political advantage. Rather, they tended to be serious efforts to understand the *why* behind the results, and they focused on management issues rarely discussed in the popular press. There were reports, for example, on how a city's failure to have a modern and effective information technology system made a difference to the city's citizens. There were stories about the difficulties of hiring in a rigid personnel system, about effectively measuring performance, and about whether making the government's budget available in libraries was the most effective way of allowing citizen access. These implications of management in the daily practice of government are very important but are rarely explored.

Second, governments and government agencies clearly treated this grading exercise as a learning opportunity and an incentive to do better. Many, at all the levels studied by the projects, reported that the process itself was helpful because it subjected them to an external evaluation of systems and practices that were often "under the radar." Moreover, many saw the opportunity to be recognized for management success as a welcome change from the negative coverage more common in the media, as well as an opportunity to begin a discussion and debate with legislators and others reluctant to engage in discussion of government's daily operations.

Third, governments and agencies clearly sought out lesson-learning opportunities. Some well-managed federal agencies, for example, conducted what is best described as a "tour" of other agencies after the release of the FPP stories; agency managers were interested knowing what they could learn from others. One city posted their survey and accompanying materials on the Web after requests from other cities and other interested parties strained staffs' ability to respond. Moreover, GPP and FPP staff frequently provided more detailed briefings to key government and agency staff, giving those organizations access to a broader and more in-depth analysis of their management.

Linkages to Other Research and to Other Capacity-Building Activity

At the time the GPP was designed and implemented and since, there have been three major developments in related research and management oriented activities. First, concurrent with the broad international focus on governance, there emerged a strong academic and institutional interest on capacity broadly writ; that is, on the ability to effectively govern (Peters and Savoie, 1999; Pollitt and Bouckaert, 2000). Organizations such as the World Bank and the Organization for Economic Cooperation and Development moved from more narrow reform and change efforts to this capacity-building focus (OECD, 2001; Holmes, 1996). As a result, the components of institutional capacity building, including management systems and support, were increasingly viewed as policy tools.

Second, there was an increasing awareness that the management systems of government were in some disarray. The Y2K "crisis" made the point quite clearly in relation to information technology. At the same time, the ability of governments and their agencies to respond both strategically and effectively to this crisis increased the awareness of the potential that could be unleashed when change was both necessary and supported.

More recently, the GAO has sounded the alarm about a specific management system: human resource management. Noting that "inattentiveness to strategic human capital management has created a government-wide risk—one that is fundamental to the federal government's ability to effectively serve the American people," the GAO placed human resource management on its government-wide high risk list (GAO, 2001b: 72). Building capacity *within* each of the management systems the projects analyzed, therefore, has assumed a broader and more intense focus.

The third major linkage to other research and reform activities is through the complex connections between capacity, performance, and governance. The discussion of the GPP/FPP conceptual model presented in Chapter 2 laid out the capacity-performance linkages as we assumed they existed. In that model, management capacity is viewed as the "middle of the performance equation," that is, as a necessary (but not sufficient) precondition for improved performance. Research and analysis focusing specifically on welfare-to-work programs, which is now underway at Manpower Development Research Corporation (MDRC) makes the same assumption but specifically links management and other organizational characteristics to performance as measured by individual level outcomes (Riccio, Bloom, and Hill, 2000).

Related work by Heinrich and Lynn and others explicitly includes both performance and governance in the underlying conceptual model, called "the logic of governance" (Heinrich and Lynn, 2000). For the last five years, in academic conferences at Arizona's School of Business and Public Policy, Syracuse University's Maxwell School of Public Affairs, and Texas A&M's Bush School, these themes have been pursued by a small group of academics whose research activities address the themes through different lenses.* The emerging research in this area is promising for its focus on institutional arrangements, on specific links to performance and performance measure-

*See Meier and O'Toole, 2001; O'Toole and Meier, 1999; Jennings and Ewalt, 2000; Heinrich and Lynn, 2000; Heinrich, 2000; Heinrich and Lynn, 2001; Lynn, Heinrich, Hill, 2000; Milward and Provan, 1995 and 2000; Provan and Milward, 2001; Ingraham and Kneedler, 2000a and 2000b.

ment, and on the critical links between performance and governance. All of these comprise significant components of public management reform design, an activity based too often in the past on private sector models or otherwise untested experiments. The potential contributions to the practical world of policymaking are very significant.

Finally, a body of research that specifically plants management capacity at the middle of the equation and explores links to specific but different measures of performance is also emerging. Recent work by Coggburn and Schneider (2001) explores the relationship between political and environmental influences, management capacity, and the broad policy choices states make. Brudney and Wright (2001) use a capacity variable to examine states' efforts in reinvention reforms. Other work explores capacity links to specific policy choices, such as those related to building and using rainy-day funds (Hou, Moynihan, and Ingraham, forthcoming) and use of performance information (Joyce and Tompkins, 2002). Not all analysts agree with the focus, of course, but a healthy debate has been engaged (Kirlin, 2001).

Research Agenda for the Future

As is often the case with research, the process of making progress has succeeded in clarifying critical gaps in our knowledge and has demonstrated the enormous progress yet to be made. There is a great deal that we as a community of public management analysts still do not know. There are a number of avenues for additional research to be followed by scholars who wish either to build on the work of the GPP/FPP or to proceed in other fruitful directions.

1. **Linking Management and Performance.** As we noted in both Chapter 1 and this chapter, our overarching goal in the GPP/FPP projects has been to make progress in measuring management and in clarifying its role in the performance equation. We have asserted that, all else being equal, a well-managed government or agency will have better potential for high performance than will a poorly managed organization. While it would be desirable to be more rigorously specific about the contribution of management (versus political and environmental factors, for example) to policy outcomes, significant steps have been taken, and the research agenda in this regard has become much more clear.

Donahue's detailed study links management to overall results in fire departments (1999, 2000, and 2001). Heinrich's work (2000), as well as that of Meier and O'Toole (2001), with structure is also important. Brudney and Wright's (2001) efforts to specifically link good management to the ability to engage in other reform-oriented activities represents another direction for future research. Meier and O'Toole (2001) have also developed a measure of managerial skill and have found that quality management contributes positively to public program performance.

2. **Understanding How Management Matters.** Even understanding that management matters, and how much, does not tell us in what ways it matters. Here there are two significant additional areas for research. First, it is important to know which components of management are likely to be most significant. Does financial management matter more than human resource management? Does managing for results matter more than any of the other systems, or is it necessary to have effectively managed base management systems in order to attempt results-based management?

Second, it is important to identify which components of management and management systems are most amenable to policy change or reform. Emphasizing that something is "important" is not the same as saying that it is amenable to change. Nonetheless, the GPP and FPP have substantially enhanced our understanding of how similar policies work in different settings. Despite the presence of national standards for some systems, such as financial management, management reforms are not of the "one size fits all" variety. Understanding the capacity for change in different environments and political settings is important to creating longer-term effectiveness. Comparative case studies of similar policies and practices in different settings could make a valuable contribution.

3. **Achieving the Strategic Balance in Centralization/Decentralization.** As we noted in the previous chapter, this research does not allow the unequivocal support of either centralized or decentralized systems, but rather emphasizes the need for careful policy design and choice. Particularly in human resource management and in information management, we often found highly decentralized systems, but—contrary to findings about the pace of change generally—we also found rapid shifts in a relatively short period of time.

Much contemporary management reform literature, notably that related to new public management, advocates discretion and flexibility, implying a movement away from centralized controls (Pollitt and Bouckaert, 2000). Our work suggests that decisions about centralization and decentralization are much more situational and multidimensional. For example, the National Weather Service was able to resolve a longstanding information technology management problem with an old-fashioned hierarchical solution. On the other hand, the Veterans Health Administration achieved management improvements by empowering its regional directors. Many states are moving away from decentralized structures—or at least imposing some "structure" on decentralization.

There are enormous differences from management system to management system in the governments and agencies we studied. It is important, therefore, to understand sets of conditions under which centralized approaches are most effective and cases in which decentralized efforts will have a greater payoff. That is not yet clear.

4. Exploring "Grounded Leadership" More Fully. Despite the fact that we had not initially intended to study leadership—indeed, were advised not to do so—leadership surfaced as an important influence in the effective governments we studied. It was notably absent in those governments not doing so well. Even in the preliminary analyses presented here, we found that strong leadership in public organizations was most often best described as a team effort, spanning political and career staff boundaries and including short-term elected officials but also career staff with a longer-term view and understanding of the organization. We found further that these leaders and teams had the ability and the will to move from strategic vision-setting to a very practical view of making the vision happen. This included a willingness to be involved with implementation and to oversee implementation activities.

Leadership was somewhat situational, in the sense that effective leaders and leadership teams captured opportunities for change or created them if necessary. One consistent characteristic of strong leaders and teams, however, was a sound organizational base. Understanding the organization and the management capacities it required well enough to foster and sustain effective system creation was central. We called this leadership model "grounded leadership" (Ingraham, 2001).

But the idea of grounded leadership needs fuller development. The concept as we have presented it here is particularly appropriate to the public sector. A leader or team grounded in systems and concerned with implementation is different in significant ways from the heroic or highly individualistic leader often described in leadership literature, most notably that associated with private sector work. The "grounded leadership" model has emerged, however, from a large and very systematic analysis of governments' operation. It may well provide the most consistent evidence of links between effective leaders and effective governments available to analysts. It clearly warrants further explanation.

Questions to be explored beyond the very preliminary analysis we were able to present here include the following: How, precisely, do "grounded" leaders operate? How do they make the connections between vision and the administrative actions and capabilities necessary to make good on that vision? Where do they come from? Is there a particular time frame in which the capacity building block activities described elsewhere in this book must occur? How, in an institutional context, does the leader or the team "seize the moment"? Are there patterns regarding where the leaders come from and the backgrounds they need in order to be effective in a public setting?

5. Exploring Comparative Application of Lessons Learned. The projects have focused on states, cities, and federal agencies over the first full three years. In year 4, the focus was expanded to counties and additional federal agencies. Some potential conclusions can be reached about management by level and type of government thus far. For example, because well-managed local governments tend to have a greater degree of goal clarity, their pursuit of results and ability to measure them may be easier.

At the same time, some governments—including most states and the federal government—have a legislative mandate to manage for results, but the reality is decidedly mixed. Under what conditions and with what specific provisions does legislation or legislative support matter? Is the impact of a legislative imprimatur different from system to system? How?

While even these lessons can and should be expanded, the project has not formally studied connections and transferability between management systems in the United States and management in the rest of the world. For example, the countries of the Organization for Economic Cooperation and Development (OECD) have been engaged in reform efforts for approximately fifteen years. Countries such as Australia, New Zealand, and the United Kingdom have a number of efforts underway to reform their management systems, including some whose base of assessment are criteria similar to those employed by the GPP and FPP (Boston, Martin, Pallot, and Walsh, 1996; Peters and Savoie, 1999). In addition, the World Bank has been pressing developing countries to engage in administrative reform initiatives. We have not, in this project, attempted to compare the lessons learned from the U.S. effort to management lessons from other countries. Given the nature of contemporary policy diffusion, such analyses would be a logical and very important area for further inquiry.

6. Exploring Connections Between Innovation and Systemic Capacity. Governments and government agencies are often slow to change and, for many reasons, are vested in the status quo. This has been well documented in the literature (Meier, 1993; Pressman and Wildavsky, 1984). For at least the

last decade, however, there has been a strong emphasis on greater "risk-taking" and innovation in government (Osborne and Gaebler, 1992; NPR, 1993b and 1997). Innovation, sadly, does not necessarily lead to either positive or long-term change. While we can say anecdotally that many governments or agencies that attempted to challenge conventional administrative practice saw positive results, there are also cases in which both innovation and real change were fleeting. Although, as noted in the last chapter, we found receptivity to learning as well as a clear awareness that the learning curve for change was often lengthy, we did not systematically study the relationship of innovation to the development of longer-term systemic management capacity. Exploring this linkage is not only a fruitful but also a necessary area for further inquiry.

7. **Exploring Significance of Clarity of Task and Authority to Manage.** One of the significant constraints to management that has been identified in the U.S. context is the general lack of clarity for managers. Because of the fragmented nature of the political system, agencies and agency managers lack clear direction on appropriate policies or priorities to pursue. They also confront multiple and sometimes conflicting oversight mechanisms as well as different budgetary timelines. "Clarity of task and purpose" (Holmes, 1996) has been identified as crucial to results-based reform efforts in other countries but tends not to be present in the United States, particularly at the state and national levels. We found this to be a major challenge, especially in our evaluation of some federal agencies. More work needs to be done, however, in measuring clarity of purpose and identifying its particular significance in terms of the ability of programs or agencies to measure and achieve results. Many of these problems are, of course, political and emanate from the desire of elected officials for extensive oversight and specific constituent services as well as from the desires of citizens to have very specific and narrow needs addressed in broad public programs. Nonetheless, if the practice of being all things to all people means essentially that public organizations cannot perform effectively—and our research demonstrates this to be true in many cases—alternative scenarios deserve some consideration.

8. **Relating Management to Context.** One of the key contributions of the academic-journalistic collaboration in this project was to ensure attention to the context in which these governments or agencies managed. Particular attention was paid to the political context—the role of legislative bodies and elected chief executive in setting the direction or (perhaps as frequently) setting out roadblocks that make it more difficult to progress. We are, however, only beginning to look at context in a systematic way (Dona-

hue, Selden, and Ingraham, 2000; Hou, Moynihan, and Ingraham, forth-coming). Nor have we looked carefully at contextual factors not related to politics—socioeconomic factors and the nature of agency mission at the federal level, for example. A more thorough understanding of the contextual setting in which management occurs can contribute to identifying where "improvements" are likely to be most or least successful—or when threshold conditions for change are likely to be present.

9. **Using Performance Information for Management and Policy.** Many governments have gotten the performance measurement message, in the sense that they have moved aggressively toward identifying outcomes for their programs and measuring progress toward them. The next great challenge for them is using that information to make decisions and policy. In particular, the use of performance information in the budget process is the next significant step in the movement toward performance management. Understanding how performance information and the budget process can be connected is getting greater attention (See Hilton and Joyce, 2003), but there are very few studies that evaluate how performance information is actually being used in the budget process (Joyce and Tompkins, 2002; Moynihan and Ingraham, 2001a).

A related issue is the challenge of trying to understand theoretically and empirically the linkages between organizational performance, individual performance, and the incentives for both. The GPP and FPP focused only on broad organizational performance issues, but obviously many of the governments and agencies we studied have struggled valiantly with issues of individual performance and reward. More systematic and detailed study is necessary, however, if performance is to be more fully understood and incentives for achieving it more properly aligned.

10. **Using Management Information to Teach.** The lessons learned from the GPP and FPP will have more lasting currency if they are communicated to students of public administration/public policy in ways that highlight their relevance to practice and their relationship to broader conceptual issues. The best way to accomplish this is through the development of good teaching cases. There is a serious need for cases that focus on management transformations in government or organizations, but that also describe success. One of the enduring lessons of the GPP/FPP is that there are many successful leaders and management teams in public organizations; their experiences belong in the classroom. The key will be to structure these cases in a way that brings the real management challenges and solutions to life.

Conclusion

The GPP and the FPP represent the largest assessment of public management capacity ever undertaken in the United States. In providing a broad, detailed, and comprehensive description of management structures, processes, and activities across many governments and at multiple levels, the projects have provided an important foundation for future theory development and even further refinement of evaluative criteria. And they have generated new testable hypotheses, which highlight opportunities for targeted empirical investigation.

The projects' success depended on the participation and engagement of public officials too numerous to count at every level of government studied. The lessons we learned transform the century-old public administration nostrum—"Of course management matters"—into a set of nuanced conclusions and sensible speculation about both public organizations and the managers and leaders who inhabit them. The conclusions also challenge many of the negative stereotypes so common in the United States: in fairness, the "bad old bureaucrat" looks more like a committed problem solver in many cases. Both the GPP and the FPP found many examples of very good management and of constantly learning organizations.

The American system is a harsh one for public managers. Expectations for service delivery are high—frequently unrealistically so. Purpose and mission for programs contain conflicting and sometimes contradictory objectives. Trust in public managers and other public servants is low. Interest is much higher in building controls than in building capacity. And yet performance—more bang for the taxpayers' buck—is a high priority.

The context is daunting. But the experience and the efforts that the GPP and the FPP chronicled are more positive. There is much good management in government, sometimes against significant odds. Furthermore, in spite of the difficult jobs that confront them, governments and agencies want to do better and actively seek opportunities to learn how.

The movement toward better performance offers such an opportunity. It will pay off. How long this will take depends on a number of factors. High on this list will be the point we have emphasized throughout this book: Expectations for performance should be tailored to the real capacity of governments to perform, and this capacity must be created. If the capacity is not there or is not created, better performance is a pipe dream. Of course, both governments and agencies must take the effort seriously and must be given incentives to do so. Elected officials must work to create and sustain a setting that is conducive to performance. There are many examples of success at all levels of government in meeting these challenges and moving ahead. As this book demonstrates, questions remain about precise maps for specific cases. But clearly, understanding the conditions for performance—and not simply promising to achieve it—is a critical first step.

Appendixes

Government Performance Project
MPA Research Staff Assistants, 1996–2002

1996–1997

Peter Forsberg
Bruce Jones
Amy Schmit
Susan Seig Tompkins

1997–1998

Anand Aidasani
Matthew Beekman
Mike Berfield
Megan Carroll
Don Moynihan
Susan Seig Tompkins

1998–1999

Thomas Cook
Geoffrey Green
Louis Heinzer
Jessalynn Kearney
Kyle Kotary
Daniel Prather
Anthony Stacy
Amy Westpfahl
Kristen Wollenhaupt

1999–2000

Mark Birnbaum
Leslie Carsman
Felipe Colon

Nicole Diamantes
Jim Fleming
Kelly Gavin
Christina Higdon
Maja Husar
Kristin Lieser
Ellen Rubin
Baljit Samra
Tom Sather
Bernard Schulz
Dinka Spirovska
Tayyab Walker

2000–2001

Sarah Chapman
Amy Choi
Dominic Cloud
Jessica Crawford
Miguel Elizalde
Figen Gungor
Min Lee
Jennifer Parmalee
Fabian Ramirez
Tiffany Tanner
Roxana Tiron
Dan Tompkins
Rajesh Vasudevan

2001–2002

Paula Acosta
Korey Adams
Edward Angley
Jason Bakelar
Lisa Brown
Elizabeth Callender
Catherine Choi
Margaret Dobrydnio
Kate Gilpin
Rebecca Hall
Yao Huang
Melissa Mink
LeeAnne Rogers
Martin Skahen
Martha Wilson

Government Performance Project Senior Advisory Board

Mark O. Hatfield, Chair
Reubin Askew
David Birnbaum
Constance Berry Newman
John Norquist

Federal Performance Project
Research and Grading Assistance, 2000–2002

2000–2001 *Research Assistants*

Alan Alvarez
Antonia Edwardson
Julie Middleton
Amy Rofman
Suzanne Summers

2001–2002 *Research Assistants*

Sarah Fabrikiewicz
Amanda Hazelwood
Cesar Rodriquez
Noah Wepman
Melissa Zimmerman

2001 *Grading Advisory Board*

Kenneth Apfel
G. Edward DeSeve
Renato Dipentima
Mortimer L. Downey
Steven Kelman
Susan Robinson King
C. Morgan Kinghorn

2002 *Grading Advisory Board*

G. Edward DeSeve
Renato Dipentima
Mortimer L. Downey
J Christopher Mihm
Hannah Sistare
A. W. "Pete" Smith

Appendix 3.1. Federal Agency Management Assessment Criteria

Managing for Results

Performance Measurement

1. Does the agency have a clearly articulated statement of its mission, and does it understand how its activities drive mission success? Does this mission understanding extend vertically throughout the organization?
2. Are the measures of success focused (at least in part) on outcomes? Are the measures related to the mission and goals as reflected in the strategic plan? Does the agency have a balanced set of measures?
3. Are performance data reliable?
4. Are appropriate measures reported to individuals at different levels of the organization, and to external stakeholders?
5. Are performance measures used to influence and/or inform resource allocation decisions? To what extent are there individual or group incentives to contribute to organizational performance?

Strategic Planning

1. Does the planning process in the agency involve relevant stakeholders, employees, etc.?
2. Are priorities determined in a systematic way that evaluates the contribution of different policies or actions to the achievement of the agency's mission?
3. Is there a clear crosswalk between the strategic plan and measures of performance? Does actual performance inform future planning decisions?
4. Is there a clear interface between planning and budgeting processes?

Agency Management

1. To what extent do line managers have in allocating resources within their organizations? To what extent do they have the ability to change processes to increase agency productivity?
2. To what extent are managers held accountable for agency performance?
3. Does the agency use program evaluation to determine opportunities for improvement and to test assumptions about the effects of programs?

Contributions of Other Management Systems

Human Resources Management

1. Does the agency have sufficient numbers of people, with the right skills and abilities to carry out the mission of the agency?
2. Is the agency able to allocate its personnel, by mission or geographically, in a way that maximizes its ability to achieve its mission?
3. Does the agency engage in workforce planning that is designed to determine future human resource requirements, and are employees and stakeholders involved in these planning efforts?
4. To what extent does the agency provide line managers with the capability to hire, fire, reward and train the people that work for them?

Information Management

1. Do employees have the information they need, provided in a timely manner, to effectively carry out the mission of the agency?
2. Does the agency have the capacity to determine whether the information provided is sufficient and timely?
3. To what extent are decisions on procuring additional information resources related to requirements necessary to enable the agency to better achieve results?
4. Does information about agency operations and performance flow vertically and horizontally through the agency, as well as to external stakeholders?
5. Does the agency, to the extent practicable, make use of electronic solutions in providing services or information to the people that it serves?

Physical Asset Management

1. Do employees have sufficient equipment and facilities to effectively carry out the mission of the agency?
2. To what extent does the agency track the status, availability and condition of its physical assets?
3. Is the process of allocating resources for replacement, maintenance, and acquisition of new physical assets clearly related to mission success, following the OMB Capital Programming Guide or some similar performance-based guidance?

Financial Management

1. Is the agency's determination of necessary funding, and subsequent allocation of that funding across agency subunits, related to its ability to best achieve its strategic goals?
2. Do agency managers receive timely and accurate information on budgeted funds?

3. Does the agency track activity costs (in a way that enables them to tie marginal costs to marginal performance), and if so, how is this done?

4. Did the agency receive an unqualified opinion on its most recent audited financial statements, or (in cases where statements are prepared at a higher level) were shortcomings noted in Department financial statements a result of the agency's financial weaknesses?

Appendix 3.2. State Government Management Assessment Criteria

Financial Management

1. Government has a multi-year perspective on budgeting.
   - Government produces meaningful current revenue and expenditure estimates.
   - Government produces meaningful future revenue and expenditure forecasts.
   - Government can gauge the future fiscal impact of financial decisions.
2. Government has mechanisms that preserve stability and fiscal health.
   - Government's budget reflects a structural balance between ongoing revenues and expenditures.
   - Government uses countercyclical or contingency planning devices effectively.
   - Government appropriately manages long-term liabilities, including pension funds.
   - Government appropriately uses and manages debt.
   - Government's investment and cash management practices appropriately balance return & solvency.
3. Sufficient financial information is available to policymakers, managers, and citizens.
   - Government produces accurate, reliable, and thorough financial reports.
   - Useful financial data is available to government managers.
   - Government communicates budgetary and financial data to citizens.
   - Government produces financial reports in a timely manner.
   - Government is able to gauge the cost of delivering programs or services.
   - Government budget is adopted on time.
4. Government has appropriate control over financial operations.
   - Government balances sufficient control over expenditures with sufficient managerial flexibility.
   - Government effectively manages procurement, including contracts for delivery of goods & services.

Human Resources Management

1. Government conducts strategic analysis of present and future human resource needs.

- Government has sufficient data about its workforce to support analysis.
- Government plans ahead to meet its future workforce needs.
2. Government is able to obtain the employees they need.
    - Government hires employees in a timely manner.
    - Government managers have appropriate discretion in the hiring process.
    - Government conducts effective recruiting efforts.
    - Government hires appropriately skilled and qualified employees.
3. Government is able to maintain an appropriately skilled workforce.
    - Government conducts appropriate training to develop and maintain employee skills.
    - Government is able to retain skilled and experienced employees.
    - Government is able to discipline employees.
    - Government is able to terminate employees.
4. Government is able to motivate employees to perform effectively in support of the government's goals.
    - Government is able to reward superior performance through pay and other cash/non-cash incentives.
    - Government is able to evaluate the performance of its employees effectively.
    - Sufficient opportunity for employee feedback exists.
    - Government is able to maintain productive labor-management relations.
5. Government has a civil service structure that supports its ability to achieve its workforce goals.
    - Government's classifications system is coherent and of the appropriate size.
    - Government personnel policies permit appropriate flexibility in the civil service and pay structures.
    - Government's human resources goals and policies are communicated to employees.

Information Technology Management

1. Government-wide and agency-level information technology systems provide information that adequately supports managers' needs and strategic goals.
2. Government's information technology systems form a coherent architecture.
    - Strategies are in place to support present and future coherence in architecture.
3. Government conducts meaningful, multi-year information technology planning.
    - Information technology planning process is centralized.
    - Government managers have appropriate input into the planning process.
    - Formal government-wide and agency information technology plans exist.

4. Information technology training is adequate.
   - Information technology end-users are adequately trained to use available systems.
   - Information technology specialists are adequately trained to operate available systems.
5. Government can evaluate and validate the extent to which information technology system benefits justify investment.
6. Governments can procure the information technology systems they need in a timely manner.
7. IT systems support the government's ability to communicate with and provide services to its citizens.

Capital Management

1. Government conducts thorough analysis of future needs.
   - Government has a formal capital plan that coordinates and prioritizes capital activities.
   - A multi-year linkage between operating and capital budgeting exists.
   - A multi-year linkage between strategic planning and capital budgeting exists.
   - Government has sufficient data to support analysis.
2. Government monitors and evaluates projects throughout their implementation.
3. Government conducts appropriate maintenance of capital assets.
   - Government has sufficient data to plan maintenance adequately.
   - Maintenance is appropriately funded.

Managing For Results

1. Government engages in results-oriented, strategic planning.
   - Strategic objectives and identified and provide a clear purpose.
   - Government leadership effectively communicates the strategic objectives to all employees.
   - Government plans are responsive to input from citizens and other stakeholders, including employees.
   - Agency plans are coordinated with central government plans.
2. Government develops indicators and evaluative data that can measure progress toward results.
   - Government can ensure that data is valid and accurate.
3. Leaders and managers use results data for policymaking, management, and evaluation of progress.
4. Government clearly communicates the results of its activities to stakeholders.

Appendix 3.3. Local Government Management Assessment Criteria

Financial Management Criteria

1. Government has a multi-year perspective on budgeting.
   - Government produces meaningful current revenue and expenditure estimates.
   - Government produces meaningful future revenue and expenditure forecasts.
   - Government can gauge the future fiscal impact of financial decisions.
2. Government has mechanisms that preserve stability and fiscal health.
   - Government's budget reflects a structural balance between ongoing revenues and expenditures.
   - Government uses countercyclical or contingency planning devices effectively.
   - Government appropriately manages long-term liabilities, including pension funds.
   - Government appropriately uses and manages debt.
   - Government's investment and cash management practices appropriately balance return & solvency.
3. Sufficient financial information is available to policymakers, managers, and citizens.
   - Government produces accurate, reliable, and thorough financial reports.
   - Useful financial data is available to government managers.
   - Government communicates budgetary and financial data to citizens.
   - Government produces financial reports in a timely manner.
   - Government is able to gauge the cost of delivering programs or services.
   - Government budget is adopted on time.
4. Government has appropriate control over financial operations.
   - Government exercises sufficient control over expenditures.
   - Government permits sufficient managerial flexibility.
   - Government effectively manages procurement, including contracts for delivery of goods and services.

Human Resources Management Criteria

1. Government conducts strategic analysis of present and future human re-
   source needs.
   - Government has sufficient data about its workforce to support analysis.
   - Government plans ahead to meet its future workforce needs.
2. Government is able to obtain the employees it needs.
   - Government hires employees in a timely manner.
   - Government managers have appropriate discretion in the hiring process.
   - Government conducts effective recruiting efforts.
   - Government hires appropriately skilled and qualified employees.
3. Government is able to maintain an appropriately skilled workforce.
   - Government conducts appropriate training to develop and maintain em-
     ployee skills.
   - Government is able to retain skilled and experienced employees.
   - Government is able to discipline employees.
   - Government is able to terminate employees.
4. Government is able to motivate employees to perform effectively in support
   of the government's goals.
   - Government is able to reward superior performance through pay and
     other cash/non-cash incentives.
   - Government is able to evaluate the performance of its employees effec-
     tively.
   - Sufficient opportunity for employee feedback exists.
   - Government is able to maintain productive labor-management relations.
5. Government has a civil service structure that supports its ability to achieve its
   workforce goals.
   - Government's classifications system is coherent and of the appropriate size.
   - Government personnel policies permit appropriate flexibility in the civil
     service and pay structures.
   - Government's human resources goals and policies are communicated to
     employees.

Information Technology Management Criteria

1. Government-wide and agency-level information technology systems provide
   information that adequately supports managers' needs and strategic goals.
2. Government's information technology systems form a coherent architecture.
   - Strategies are in place to support present and future coherence in architec-
     ture.
3. Government conducts meaningful, multi-year information technology planning.

- Information technology planning process is centralized.
- Government managers have appropriate input into the planning process.
- Formal government-wide and agency information technology plans exist.
4. Information technology training is adequate.
   - Information technology end-users are adequately trained to use available systems.
   - Information technology specialists are adequately trained to operate available systems.
5. Government can evaluate and validate the extent to which IT system benefits justify investment.
6. Governments can procure the information technology systems they need in a timely manner.
7. IT systems support the government's ability to communicate with and provide services to its citizens.

Capital Management Criteria

1. Government conducts thorough analysis of future needs.
   - Government has a formal capital plan that coordinates and prioritizes capital activities.
   - A multi-year linkage between operating and capital budgeting exists.
   - A multi-year linkage between strategic planning and capital budgeting exists.
   - Government has sufficient data to support analysis.
2. Government monitors and evaluates projects throughout their implementation.
3. Government conducts appropriate maintenance of capital assets.
   - Government has sufficient data to plan maintenance adequately.
   - Maintenance is appropriately funded.

Managing For Results

1. Government engages in results-oriented, strategic planning.
   - Government leadership effectively communicates the strategic vision to all employees.
   - Government plans are responsive to input from citizens and other stakeholders.
   - Agency plans are coordinated with central government plans.
2. Government develops indicators and evaluative data that can measure progress toward results and accomplishments.
   - Government can ensure that data is valid and accurate.
3. Leaders and managers use results data for policymaking, management, and evaluation of progress.
4. Government clearly communicates the results of its activities to stakeholders.

Appendix 4.1. Cities, Counties, and Federal Agencies Graded

Cities

Anchorage (AK)
Atlanta (GA)
Austin (TX)
Baltimore (MD)
Boston (MA)
Buffalo (NY)
Chicago (IL)
Cleveland (OH)
Columbus (OH)
Dallas (TX)
Denver (CO)
Detroit (MI)
Honolulu (HI)
Houston (TX)
Indianapolis (IN)
Jacksonville (FL)
Kansas City (MO)
Long Beach (CA)
Los Angeles (CA)
Memphis (TN)
Milwaukee (WI)
Minneapolis (MN)
Nashville (TN)
New Orleans (LA)
New York City (NY)
Philadelphia (PA)
Phoenix (AZ)
Richmond (VA)
San Antonio (TX)
San Diego (CA)
San Francisco (CA)
San Jose (CA)
Seattle (WA)
Virginia Beach (VA)
Washington (DC)

Counties*

West Region
Alameda (CA)
Clark (NV)
Contra Costa (CA)
King (WA)
Los Angeles (CA)
Maricopa (AZ)
Orange (CA)
Riverside (CA)
Sacramento (CA)
San Bernardino (CA)
San Diego (CA)
Santa Clara (CA)

South Region
Broward (FL)
Dallas (TX)
Fairfax (VA)
Fulton (GA)
Harris (TX)
Hillsborough (FL)
Mecklenburg (NC)
Metro Dade (FL)
Palm Beach (FL)
Shelby (TN)

Midwest Region
Cook (IL)
Cuyahoga (OH)
Franklin (OH)
Hamilton (OH)
Hennepin (MN)
Milwaukee (WI)
Oakland (MI)
Wayne (MI)

Northeast Region
Allegheny (PA)
Anne Arundel (MD)
Baltimore (MD)
Erie (NY)
Monroe (NY)
Montgomery (MD)
Nassau (NY)
Prince Georges (MD)
Suffolk (NY)
Westchester (NY)

Federal Agencies

1999
Customs Service
Environmental Protection
  Agency
Federal Aviation Admin-
  istration
Federal Emergency
  Management Agency

*The full analyses of the counties and the 2002 federal agencies were not completed as of the time of this writing and so are not included in our discussion.

Federal Housing Administration

Food and Drug Administration

Food and Nutrition Service

Food Safety and Inspection Service

Health Care Financing Administration

Immigration and Naturalization Service

Internal Revenue Service

Occupational Safety and Health Administration

Patent and Trademark Office

Social Security Administration

Veterans Health Administration

2000

Army Corps of Engineers

Coast Guard

National Park Service

Office of Student Financial Assistance

Veterans Benefits Administration

2001

Administration for Children and Families

Bureau of Consular Affairs

Bureau of Indian Affairs

Forest Service

National Aeronautics and Space Administration

National Weather Service

Postal Service

2002*

Centers for Medicare and Medicaid Services

Environmental Protection Agency

Federal Aviation Administration

Immigration and Naturalization Service

Internal Revenue Service

Social Security Administration

References

Abramson, Mark. 1989. "The Leadership Factor." *Public Administration Review* 49(6): 562–65.

Ammar, Salwa, and Ronald Wright. 2000. "Ranking State Financial Management: A Multilevel Fuzzy Rule-based System." *Decision Sciences* 31(2): 449–52.

Anthony, Robert, and David Young. 1999. *Management Control in Nonprofit Organizations,* 6th ed. New York: Irwin/McGraw Hill.

Bardach, Eugene. 2000. *A Practical Guide for Policy Analysis: The Eightfold Path to More Effective Problem Solving.* New York: Chatham House.

Barrett, Katherine, and Richard Greene. 1999. "Grading the States." *Governing* 12(5): 17–90.

———. 1995. "State of the States 1995." *Financial World* 39(6): 36–60.

Barzelay, Michael, and Babak Armajani. 1991. *Breaking Through Bureaucracy: A New Vision for Managing in Government.* Berkeley: University of California Press.

Bass, Bernard. 1985. *Leadership and Performance Beyond Expectations.* New York: Free Press.

Bavon, Aloysius. 1995. "Innovation in Performance Measurement Systems: A Comparative Perspective." *International Journal of Public Administration* 18(2 and 3): 491–519.

Behn, Robert. 1991. *Leadership Counts.* Cambridge, Mass.: Harvard University Press.

Borins, Sanford. 2000. "Loose Cannons and Rule Breakers or Enterprising Leaders? Some Evidence About Innovative Public Managers." *Public Administration Review* 60:489–509.

Boston, Jonathan, John Martin, June Pallot, and Pat Walsh. 1996. *Public Management: The New Zealand Model.* Auckland, New Zealand: Oxford University Press.

Bozeman, Barry, and Stuart Bretschneider. 1986. "Public Management Information Systems: Theory and Prescription." *Public Administration Review* 46 (Special Issue): 475–87.

Bretschneider, Stuart I., and Wilpen L. Gorr. 1987. "State and Local Revenue Forecasting." In *The Handbook of Forecasting,* edited by Spyros Makridakis and Steven Wheelwright. New York: John Wiley.

Broderick, Melissa, Brian Jacob, and Anthony Bryk. 2000. "The Impact of High Stakes Testing in Chicago on Student Achievement in Promotional Gate Grades." Paper presented at the Association for Public Policy Analysis and

Management Annual Research Conference. November 2–4, Seattle, Washington.

Broom, Cheryle, and Lynn McGuire. 1995. "Performance-Based Government Models: Building a Track Record." *Public Budgeting and Finance* 15(4): 3–17.

Brudney, Jeffrey L., and Deil S. Wright. 2001. "Privatization Across the American States: Assessing and Explaining the Role of Contracting by State Administrative Agencies." Paper presented at the 2001 Annual Meeting of the American Political Science Association, San Francisco, Calif., August 30–September 2.

Coggburn, Jerrell D., and Saundra K. Schneider. 2001. "The Quality of Management and the Performance of Government: An Empirical Analysis of the American States." Paper presented at the 2001 Annual Meeting of the American Political Science Association, San Francisco, Calif., August 30–September 2.

Cohen, Steven. 1993. "Defining and Measuring Effectiveness in Public Management." *Public Productivity and Management Review* 17(1): 45–57.

Cohen, Steven, and Eimicke, William. 1995. *The New Effective Public Manager: Achieving Success in a Changing Government.* San Francisco, Calif.: Jossey-Bass.

Doig, J. M., and E. C. Hargrove, eds. 1990. *Leadership and Innovation: Entrepreneurs in Government.* Baltimore: Johns Hopkins University Press.

Donahue, Amy K. 2001. "Modeling and Measuring: The Contribution of Organizations and Management to Government Productivity, with an Application to the Fire Service." Paper presented at the Association of Budgeting and Financial Management Conference, October 5–7, 2000. Kansas City, Missouri.

———. 2000. "Putting Out Fires in Local Government: Modeling and Measuring the Influence of Managers on Public Production, with an Application to Fire Protection." Ph.D. diss. Syracuse University.

———. 1999. "Perceptions, Production, and Performance: Analysis of Public Management in the Fire Service." Paper presented at the Association for Public Policy Analysis and Management Annual Research Conference, November 4–6, Washington, D.C.

Donahue, Amy K., Sally Coleman Selden, and Patricia W. Ingraham. 2000. "Measuring Government Management Capacity: A Comparative Analysis of City Human Resources Management Systems." *Journal of Public Administration Research and Theory* 10(2): 381–411.

Evans, Karen G., and Gary L. Wamsley. 1999. "Where's the Institution? Neo-institutionalism and Public Management." In *Public Management Reform and Innovation,* edited by H. George Frederickson and Jocelyn M. Johnston. Tuscaloosa: University of Alabama Press.

Ferris, Nancy. 2000. "Information is Power." *Government Executive* 32(3): 28.

Forsythe, Dall W. 1993. "Financial Management and the Reinvention of Government." *Public Productivity and Management Review* 16(4): 415–23.

Friel, Brian. 2000. "Marked Improvements." *Government Executive* (March): 86.

Gargan, John. 1968. "Consideration of Local Government Capacity." *Public Administration Review* 41:649–58.

General Accounting Office (GAO). 2001a. *Managing for Results: Federal Managers' Views on Key Management Issues Vary Widely Across Agencies.* GAO-01-597 (May 25).

———. 2001b. *High Risk Series: An Update.* GAO-01-263 (January): 72.

———. 2000. *Human Capital: A Self-Assessment Checklist for Agency Leaders.* OCG-00-146 (September 1).

———. 1997. *Government Performance and Results Act: Government-wide Implementation Will Be Uneven.* GGD-97-109 (June 2).

Goggin, Malcolm, Ann Bowman, James Lester, and Laurence O'Toole Jr. 1990. *Implementation Theory and Practice: Toward a Third Generation.* New York: Harper Collins.

Goodnow, Frank J. 1900. *Politics and Administration: A Study in Government.* New York: Russell & Russell.

Government Executive. 2001. "How We Grade." (April): 11.

———. 1999. "Drug Money." (February): 53–56.

Gramlich, Edward. 1976. "The New York City Fiscal Crisis: What Happened and What Is to Be Done?" *American Economic Review* 66(2): 415–29.

Gulick, Luther. 1937. "Notes on the Theory of Organization." In *Papers on the Science of Administration,* edited by Luther Gulick and L. Urwick. New York: Institute of Public Administration.

Gulick, Luther, and Urwick, L., eds. 1937. *Papers on the Science of Administration.* New York: Institute of Public Administration.

Halachmi, Arie, and Theo van der Krogt. 1998. "The Role of the Manager in Employee Motivation." In *Handbook of Human Resources Management in Government,* edited by Steven Condrey. San Francisco, Calif.: Jossey-Bass.

Harris, Jean. 1995. "Service Efforts and Accomplishments Standards: Fundamental Questions of an Emerging Concept." *Public Budgeting and Finance* 15(4): 18–37.

Hatry, Harry, and James Fountain. 1990. *Service Efforts and Accomplishments Reporting: Its Time Has Come, An Overview.* Norwalk, Conn.: Governmental Accounting Standards Board.

Hatry, Harry, and Joseph Wholey. 1992. "The Case for Performance Monitoring." *Public Administration Review* 52(6): 604–11.

Hays, Steven. 1998. "Staffing the Bureaucracy: Employee Recruitment and Selection." In *Handbook of Human Resources Management in Government,* edited by Steven Condrey. San Francisco, Calif.: Jossey-Bass.

Heinrich, Carolyn J. 2000. "Organizational Form and Performance: An Empirical Investigation of Nonprofit and For-profit Job-training Service Providers." *Journal of Policy Analysis and Management* 19(2): 233–61.

Heinrich, Carolyn J., and Laurence E. Lynn Jr. 2001. "Means and Ends: A Comparative Study of Empirical Methods for Investigating Governance and Performance." *Journal of Public Administration Research and Theory* 11(1): 109.

———. 2000. "Governance and Performance: The Influence of Program Structure and Management on Job Training Partnership Act Program Outcomes." In *Governance and Performance: New Perspectives,* edited by Carolyn J. Heinrich and Laurence Lynn Jr. Washington, D.C.: Georgetown University Press.

Hilton, Rita M., and Philip G. Joyce. 2003. "Performance Information and Budgeting in Historical and Comparative Perspective." In *Handbook of Public Administration.* Thousand Oaks, Calif.: Sage Publications.

Holmes, Malcolm. 1996. "Budget Reform: Experiences from the Past 15 Years." Notes for a presentation to the South African Conference on Expenditure Budget Reform, Pretoria, South Africa, 1–2 April.

Honadle, Beth Walter. 1981. "A Capacity-building Framework: A Search for Concept and Purpose." *Public Administration Review* 41:575–80.

Hou, Yilin, William Duncombe, Salwa Ammar, and Ron Wright. 2000. "A Robust Method for Evaluating Financial Management." Unpublished manuscript. The Maxwell School, Syracuse University.

Hou, Yilin, Donald Moynihan, and Patricia W. Ingraham. Forthcoming. "Capacity, Management and Performance: Exploring the Links." *American Review of Public Administration.*

Ingraham, Patricia W. 2001. "Linking Leadership to Performance in Public Organizations." Presented to Organisation for Economic Co-operation and Development: Public Management Service, Paris, June 2001.

———. 1995. *The Foundation of Merit: Public Service in American Democracy.* Baltimore: Johns Hopkins University Press.

Ingraham, Patricia W., and Amy E. Kneedler. 2000a. "Dissecting the Black Box: Toward a Model of Government Management Performance." In *Advancing Public Management: New Developments in Theory, Methods, and Practice,* edited by Jeffrey L. Brudney, Laurence J. O'Toole Jr., and Hal G. Rainey. Washington, D.C.: Georgetown University Press.

———. 2000b. "Dissecting the Black Box Revisited: Characterizing Government Management Capacity." In *Governance and Performance: New Perspectives,* edited by Carolyn J. Heinrich and Laurence E. Lynn Jr. Washington, D.C.: Georgetown University Press.

Ingraham, Patricia W., and Donald Moynihan. 2001. "Beyond Measurement: Measuring for Results in State Government." In *Task Force on Performance Management and Measurement,* edited by R. Nathan and D. Forsythe. Rockefeller Institute, Albany, New York.

Ingraham, Patricia W., and Sally Coleman Selden. 2001. "Emerging Trends in

Human Resource Practices in the American States." In *Contemporary Issues in Human Resource Management,* 3rd ed., edited by Carolyn Ban and Norma Riccucci. New York: Longmans.

Ingraham, Patricia W., Jessica E. Sowa, and Donald P. Moynihan. 2002. "Public Sector Integrative Leadership: Linking Leadership to Performance in Public Organizations." Paper presented at the Research Workshop on the Empirical Study of Governance, Texas A&M University, College Station, Texas, February.

Ingraham, Patricia W., Sally C. Selden, Donald P. Moynihan. 2000. "People and Performance: Challenge for the Future Public Service—the Report from the Wye River Conference." *Public Administration Review* 60(1): 54–60.

Ingraham, Patricia W., James R. Thompson, Elliott F. Eisenberg. 1995. "Political Management Strategies and Political/Career Relationships: Where Are We Now in the Federal Government?" *Public Administration Review* 55:263–72.

Jacobson, Willow, Ellen Rubin, and Sally Coleman Selden. 2000. "Training in America's Largest Cities: Meeting the Needs of Tomorrow's Workforce." Campbell Public Affairs Institute Working Paper, The Maxwell School, Syracuse University.

Jennings, Edward T., and Jo Ann G. Ewalt. 2000. "Driving Caseloads Down: Welfare Policy Choices and Administrative Action in the States." In *Governance and Performance: New Perspectives,* edited by Carolyn J. Heinrich and Laurence Lynn Jr. Washington, D.C.: Georgetown University Press.

Jones, L. R. 1993. "Nine Reasons Why the CFO Act May Not Achieve its Objectives." *Public Budgeting and Finance* 13(4): 87–94.

Joyce, Philip G. 2001. "What's So Magical About Five Percent? A Nationwide Look at Factors That Influence the Optimal Size of State Rainy Day Funds." *Public Budgeting and Finance* 21(2): 62–87.

———. 1999. "Performance-Based Budgeting." In *Handbook of Government Budgeting,* edited by Roy Meyers. San Francisco, Calif.: Jossey-Bass.

———. 1993. "Using Performance Measures in the Federal Budget Process: Proposals and Prospects." *Public Budgeting and Finance* 13(4): 3–17.

Joyce, Philip G., and Susan Seig Tompkins. 2002. "Using Performance Information for Budgeting: Clarifying the Framework and Investigating Recent State Experience." In *Meeting the Challenge of Performance Oriented Government,* edited by Kathryn Newcomer et al. Washington, D.C.: American Society for Public Administration.

Jump, Bernard, Jr. 1996. "Six Easy Lessons: Learning from Orange County." *Municipal Finance Journal* 17(2): 81–94.

Kamensky, John. 1996. "Role of the 'Reinventing Government' Movement in Federal Management Reform." *Public Administration Review* 56(3): 247–55.

Kaufman, Herbert. 1965. "The Growth of the Federal Personnel System." In *Federal Government Service,* edited by Wallace Sayre. Englewood Cliff, N.J.: Prentice Hall.

Kettl, Donald. 1995. "Building Lasting Reform." In *Inside the Reinvention Machine: Appraising Government Reform*, edited by Donald Kettl and John J. DiIulio Jr. Washington, D.C.: Brookings Institution.

———. 1994. *Reinventing Government? Appraising the National Performance Review.* Washington, D.C.: Brookings Institution.

Key, V. O., Jr. 1940. "The Lack of a Budgetary Theory." *American Political Science Review* 34:1138–44.

Kirlin, John J. 2001. "Big Questions for a Significant Public Administration." *Public Administration Review* 61(2): 140–44.

Laurent, Anne. 2000. "The Curse of Can Do." *Government Executive* (March): 41–49.

Leigland, James. 1986. *WPPS: Who is to Blame for the WPPS Disaster?* New York: Public Securities Association.

Light, Paul C. 1997. *The Tides of Reform: 1945–1995.* New Haven, Conn.: Yale University Press.

———. 1999. *The True Size of Government.* Washington, D.C.: Brookings Institution.

Lynn, Laurence E. Jr. 2001. "The Myth of the Bureaucratic Paradigm: What Traditional Public Administration Really Stood For." *Public Administration Review* 61(2): 144–61.

———. 1996. *Public Management as Art, Science and Profession.* Chatham, N.J.: Chatham House.

Lynn, Laurence E., Jr., Carolyn J. Heinrich, and Carolyn J. Hill. 2001. *Improving Governance: A New Logic for Empirical Research.* Washington, D.C.: Georgetown University Press.

———. 2000. "Studying Governance and Public Management: Challenges and Prospects." *Journal of Public Administration Research and Theory* 10(2): 233–61.

———. 1999. "The Empirical Study of Governance: Theories, Models, and Methods." Prepared for a workshop on Models and Methods for the Empirical Study of Governance, University of Arizona, April 29–May 1, 1999.

Malysa, Lani Lee. 1996. "A Comparative Assessment of State Planning and Management Capacity: Tidal Wetlands Protection in Virginia and Maryland." *State and Local Government Review* 28: 205–18.

Mandell, Myrna P. 1990. "Network Management: Strategic Behavior in the Public Sector." In *Strategies for Managing Intergovernmental Policies and Networks*, edited by Robert W. Gage and Myrna P. Mandell. New York: Praeger.

McClure, David. 1997. "Improving Federal Performance in the Information Era: The Information Technology Management Improvement Reform Act of 1996." *Government Information Quarterly* 14(3): 255–69.

McIntire-Peters, Katherine. 2000. "Accounting for Success." *Government Executive* (March): 86–88.

Meier, Kenneth J. 1993. *Politics and the Bureaucracy: Policymaking in the Fourth Branch of Government*, 3rd edition. Monterey, Calif.: Brooks/Cole Publishing Company.

———. 1988. *The Political Economy of Regulation: The Case of Insurance.* Albany: State University of New York Press.

Meier, Kenneth J., and Jeff Gill. 2000. "Public Administration Research and Practice: A Methodological Manifesto." *Journal of Public Administration Research and Theory* 10(1): 157–99.

Meier, Kenneth J., and Mark Kleiman. 1995. "The Politics of Sin: Drugs, Alcohol, and Public Policy." *Journal of Policy Analysis and Management* 14(3): 473.

Meier, Kenneth J., and Deborah McFarlane. 1995. "Statutory Coherence and Policy Implementations: The Case of Family Planning." *Journal of Public Policy* 15: 281–99.

Meier, Kenneth J., and Laurence J. O'Toole Jr. 2001a. "Managerial Strategies and Behavior in Networks: A Model with Evidence from U.S. Education." *Journal of Public Administration Research and Theory* 11(3): 271.

———. 2001b. "Management in Networks: A Market Based Measure of Managerial Quality." Paper presented at the Sixth National Public Management Research Conference, October 18–21, 2001, School of Public and Environmental Affairs, Indiana University, Bloomington.

Melkers, Julia, and Katherine Willoughby. 1998. "The State of States: Performance-Based Budgeting in 47 out of 50." *Public Administration Review* 58(1): 327–34.

Meyers, Marcia K., and Nara Dillon. 1999. "Institutional Paradoxes: Why Welfare Workers Cannot Reform Welfare." In *Public Management Reform and Innovation,* edited by H. George Frederickson and Jocelyn M. Johnston. Tuscaloosa: University of Alabama Press.

Meyers, Roy T. 1997. "Is There a Key to the Normative Budgeting Lock?" *Policy Sciences* 29(3): 171–88.

Milward, H. Brinton, and Keith Provan. 2000. "Governing the Hollow State." *Journal of Public Administration Research and Theory* 10(2): 359.

———. 1995. "A Preliminary Theory of Interorganizational Network Effectiveness: A Comparative Study of Four Community Mental Health Systems." *Administrative Sciences Quarterly* 40:1–33.

Moe, Terry. 1987. "An Assessment of the Positive Theory of 'Congressional Dominance.'" *Legislative Studies Quarterly* 12: 475–520.

Moynihan, Donald P. 2000. "Managing for Results in the Cities: Report of a National Survey." Paper presented at the Annual Conference of the Western Social Science Association, San Diego, California, April 26–29, 2000.

Moynihan, Donald P., and Patricia W. Ingraham. 2001a. "Using Performance Information in Decisionmaking." Paper presented at the Public Management Research Conference, Bloomington, Indiana, October 18–20, 2001.

———. 2001b. "When Does Performance Information Contribute to Performance Information Use? Putting the Factors in Place." Campbell Public Affairs Institute Paper: 8.

Nakamura, Robert, and Frank Smallwood. 1980. *The Politics of Policy Implementation.* New York: St. Martin's Press.

National Commission on State and Local Budgeting. 1997. "Best Practices for State and Local Budgeting." Draft Report.

National Performance Review (NPR). 1997. *Businesslike Government: Lessons Learned from America's Best Companies* (Annual report). Washington, D.C.: U.S. Government Printing Office (also available at http://govinfo.library.unt.edu/npr/index.htm).

———. 1993a. *Mission Driven, Results Oriented Budgeting.* Washington, D.C.: U.S. Government Printing Office.

———. 1993b. *From Red Tape to Results: Creating a Government That Works Better and Costs Less.* Washington, D.C.: Government Printing Office.

Newcomer, Kathryn ed., 1997. *Using Performance Measurement to Improve Public and Nonprofit Programs.* San Francisco, Calif.: Jossey-Bass.

Office of Management and Budget (OMB). 1996. *Capital Programming Guide* (December 12).

O'Toole, Laurence J., Jr. 1996. "Rational Choice and the Public Management of Interorganizational Networks." In *The State of Public Management,* edited by Donald F. Kettl and H. Brinton Milward. Baltimore: Johns Hopkins University Press.

O'Toole, Laurence J., Jr., and Kenneth J. Meier. 1999. "Modeling the Impact of Public Management: Implications of Structural Context." *Journal of Public Administration Research and Theory* 9(4): 505–26.

Organisation for Economic Co-operation and Development (OECD). 2001. *Governance in the 21st Century.* Paris.

Osborne, David, and Ted Gaebler. 1992. *Reinventing Government: How the Entrepreneurial Spirit Is Transforming the Public Sector.* Reading, Mass.: Addison-Wesley.

Peters, B. Guy. 1989. *The Politics of Bureaucracy.* 3rd ed. New York: Longmans.

Peters, B. Guy, and Donald J. Savoie. 1999. *Taking Stock: Assessing Public Sector Reforms.* Montreal: McGill-Queen's University Press.

Pollitt, Christopher, and Geert Bouckaert. 2000. *Public Management Reform: A Comparative Analysis.* Oxford, U.K.: Oxford University Press.

Pressman, Jeffrey L., and Aaron Wildavsky. 1984. *Implementation.* 3rd edition, expanded. Berkeley: University of California Press.

Provan, Keith, and H. Brinton Milward. 2001. "Do Networks Really Work? A Framework for Evaluating Public-Sector Organizational Networks." *Public Administration Review* 61(4): 414.

———. 1995. "A Preliminary Theory of Interorganizational Network Effectiveness:

A Comparative Study of Four Community Mental Health Systems." *Administrative Science Quarterly* 40:1–33.

Riccio, James, Howard S. Bloom, and Carolyn J. Hill. 2000. "Management, Organizational Characteristics, and Performance: The Case of Welfare-to-Work Programs." In *Governance and Performance: New Perspectives,* edited by Carolyn J. Heinrich and Laurence E. Lynn, Jr. Washington, D.C.: Georgetown University Press.

Rodgers, Robert, and Philip Joyce. 1996. "The Effect of Underforecasting on the Accuracy of Revenue Forecasts by State Governments." *Public Administration Review* 56(1): 48–56.

Romzek, Barbara S., and Melvin J. Dubnick. 1987. "Accountability in the Public Sector: Lessons from the Challenger Tragedy." *Public Administration Review* 47(3): 227–39.

Rosenbloom, David. 2001. "History Lessons for Reinventors." *Public Administration Review* 61(2): 161–66.

———. 1993. "Have an Administrative Rx? Don't Forget the Politics!" *Public Administration Review* 53(6): 503.

———. 1989. *Public Administration: Understanding Management, Politics, and Law in the Public Sector.* New York: Random House.

Sandfort, Jodi L. 2000. "Examining the Effects of Welfare-to-Work Structures and Services on a Desired Outcome." In *Governance and Performance: New Perspectives,* edited by Carolyn J. Heinrich and Laurence E. Lynn. Washington, D.C.: Georgetown University Press.

Schwartz, Eli. 1996. "Capital Budgeting." In *Management Policies in Local Government Finance,* edited by J. Richard Aronson and Eli Schwartz, 433–45. Washington, D.C.: International City/County Management Association.

Selden, Sally C., Willow Jacobson, and Patricia W. Ingraham. 1999. "Human Resource Practices in State Governments: Findings from a National Survey." *Public Administration Review* 61(5): 598–607.

Shafritz, Jay, Walter Balk, Albert Hyde, and David Rosenbloom. 1978. *Personnel Management in Government.* Washington, D.C.: International Personnel Management Association.

Siegel, Gilbert. 1998. "Designing and Creating an Effective Compensation Plan." In *Handbook of Human Resources Management in Government,* edited by Steven Condrey. San Francisco, Calif.: Jossey-Bass.

Sobel, Russell, and Randall G. Holcombe. 1996. "The Impact of State Rainy Day Funds in Easing State Fiscal Crises During the 1990–1991 Recession." *Public Budgeting and Finance* 16(3): 28–47.

Standard and Poor's Corporation. 1986. *Debt Ratings Criteria.* New York: Standard's and Poor's Corporation.

Steinberg, Harold I. 1995. "Performance Measurement in the Federal Government: From Resources to Results." *Government Accountants Journal* 44(4): 26–30.

Taylor, Frederick Winslow. 1911. *Principles of Scientific Management*. New York: Norton.

Thompson, James. 2000. "Quasi Markets and Strategic Change in Public Organizations." In *Advancing Public Management: New Developments in Theory, Methods, and Practice*, edited by Jeffrey L. Brudney, Laurence J. O'Toole Jr., and Hal G. Rainey. Washington, D.C.: Georgetown University Press.

Tobias, Robert. 1998. "Federal Employee Unions and the Human Resources Management Function." In *Handbook of Human Resources Management in Government*, edited by Steven Condrey. San Francisco, Calif.: Jossey-Bass.

Ulrich, David, Jack Zenger, and Norman Smallwood. 1999. *Results Based Leadership*. Boston, Mass.: Harvard Business School Press.

Van Wart, Montgomery. 1998. "Organization Investment in Employee Development." In *Handbook of Human Resources Management in Government*, edited by Steven Condrey. San Francisco, Calif.: Jossey-Bass.

Waldo, Dwight. 1955. *The Study of Public Administration*. New York: Random House.

Walker, David B. 2000. "Valuing Human Capital." *Pricewaterhousecoopers Journal*. September. Washington, D.C.

Weber, Max. 1946. *From Max Weber: Essays in Sociology*. Edited by H. H. Gerth and C. Wright Mills. New York: Oxford University Press.

White, Leonard. 1926. *Introduction to the Study of Public Administration*. New York: Macmillan.

Wildavsky, Aaron. 2001. "The Politics of Budget Reform." In *The New Politics of the Budgetary Process*, 4th ed., edited by Aaron Wildavsky and Naomi Caiden. New York: Longman.

———. 1964. *The Politics of the Budgetary Process*. Boston, Mass.: Little, Brown.

Wilson, James Q. 1989. *Bureaucracy: What Government Agencies Do and Why They Do It*. New York: Basic Books.

Wilson, Woodrow. 1887. "The Study of Administration." *Political Science Quarterly* 2(1): 197–222.

Wood, B. Dan, and Jeffrey S. Peak. 1998. "The Dynamics of Foreign Policy Agenda Setting." *American Political Science Review* 92(1): 173–84.

Index

Numbers in *italics* denote figures or tables.

Cohen Act and, 111; contract management, 113; cost-benefit gaps, 41, 86; document data sources, 61; federal findings (*see* information management, federal); integration issues, 86–87, 111; Internet use in, 86–87; key purpose, 40; learning and reforms in, 141; planning in, 40–41, 85; state grades and findings, *72, 76, 84–87, 85*, 141; systems design, participation in, 41, 86; systems integration in, 86; systems modernizations, 112–13; Y2K crisis and, 111–12, 138, 141
Information Technology Management Reform Act (Clinger-Cohen Act; 1996), 42, 111
infrastructure management. *See* capital management; physical asset management, federal
innovation, 153–54
INS. *See* Immigration and Naturalization Service
integration, 20–21, 46–47; of capital management system, example, 115; challenges of, 132–33; of civil service systems, 82; evaluation of, 46–47; of financial information systems, 109; in information management, 111, 113; in information technology management, 86–87; information use and, 21, 46–47; leadership and, 20–21, 46, 133–34; and management capacity, 7, 20–21; and managing for results, 24–26, 87; in network theory, 7; and performance/management effectiveness, 20–21, 24–26
Internal Revenue Service (IRS), *95, 99*, 105, 109, 111, 123, 124, 138; Tax Systems Modernization system, 112
international systems, 153
Internet, 86–87
interviews, 59, 61–62
inventory maintenance, 116
Iowa, 88
IRS. *See* Internal Revenue Service

job classification, 83
job vacancies, 83, 103–4
journalists, as researchers, 61–62, 65, 66, 147

Kansas, 51
Kansas City, Mo., 80, 81
Kelly, Jack, 99, 113, 134
Kitzhaber, John, 132
Kizer, Kenneth, 98, 100, 132

labor-management relations, 39–40, 104–5, 137
leadership, 17–20, 131–35; evaluation of, 47–48, 54*n*; "grounded," 91, 152–53; and integration, 20–21, 24–25, 46, 133–34; and management capacity, 17–20, 117, 130; and management effectiveness/performance, 8, 17–20, 17*n*, 24–25, 47–48, 91–92, 117, 130, 131–35; in managing for results systems, 87, 98–99; and mission clarity, 131–32; and organizational strength, 130; in state and local governments, 91–92; successful practices for, 134; "vision" and, 18, 46, 87, 131–32
learning: interest in, 120, 143–44, 148; process of, 139–44
legislation, 100, 115–16, 118, 128; on managing for results, 44, 96, 129. *See also specific laws*
local governments: assessment criteria, 169–71; grading of, 65–67, 68; interviews with, 62; managing for results in, 44; in pilot study, 51; in study, 53, 172. *See also* cities; counties
Locke, Gary, 132, 133
logic, fuzzy, 65–66
"logic of governance" model, 13*n*, 149
Los Angeles, 78, 80
low-performance governments: objectives of, 142–43; response to study, 120, 143–44
Loy, Admiral James, 132, 134

maintenance, 78; of inventories, 116; link to mission, 115; link to planning, 80–81; underfunding and deferment of, 79–80, 115–16
management, 1–8, *16; vs.* administration, 5; broad lessons for, 117–20; capacity levers/dimensions of, 15–24, 27; classical ("black box") equation for, 13–14, *15;* components of, *16;* conceptual framework for, 13–24, *16*, 26–27; environ-